ESL for Job Success

On-the-Job English

Christy M. Newman

New Readers Press

On-the-Job English
ISBN 978-1-56420-147-8

Copyright © 2000 New Readers Press
New Readers Press
ProLiteracy's Publishing Division
104 Marcellus Street, Syracuse, New York 13204
www.newreaderspress.com

Printed in the United States of America
20   19   18   17   16   15   14

Proceeds from the sale of New Readers Press materials support professional
development, training, and technical assistance programs of ProLiteracy
that benefit local literacy programs in the U.S. and around the globe.

Director of Acquisition and Development: Christina Jagger
Developmental Editor: Paula L. Schlusberg
Production Director: Deborah Christiansen
Copy Editor: Julia Wittner, Judi Lauber
Design: Patricia A. Rapple
Cover Design: Kimbrly Koennecke
Illustration: Linda Tiff, Luciana Mallozzi

Contents

About This Book

Welcome to *On-the-Job English*. This book will help you build the English language skills you need to do your best at work.

In the four units that make up this book, you will develop skills in
- communicating on the job
- following safety procedures
- working with others
- using company communications

Lessons are set in places where people work in the United States—in factories and offices, in hospitals and hotels, in stores and homes. As you practice the skills presented in the lessons, think about the ways you will apply those skills in your own job. Discuss your ideas with other students, and then try the skills out at work.

Instructions for Needs Assessment and Goal Setting

Before you start this book, think about your learning needs and goals. What do you want to learn in this class? What do you need to learn for your job? The activities on pages 5–6 will help you set your goals.

Instructions for Self-Evaluation

When you finish this book, do the self-evaluation exercises on pages 123–124. The self-evaluation will help you decide what goals you reached. You will also identify the goals you still need or want to work on.

Needs Assessment and Goal Setting

Think about your needs and goals for using English at work.

How often do you need to use English for the following tasks now? What goals do you have for using English in the future? Do you need or want to reach those goals?

	Needs			Goals	
	Check (✓) one			Check (✓) one or both	
	Always	Sometimes	Never	Need	Want
1. giving and understanding instructions					
2. reading instructions or work orders					
3. scanning for information					
4. asking about instructions					
5. discussing job with supervisors					
6. discussing job with co-workers					
7. reading and using safety guidelines					
8. using safety equipment					
9. reporting problems on the job					
10. giving and getting safety warnings					
11. participating in meetings					
12. asking for and offering help					
13. expressing my opinion					
14. responding to others' opinions					
15. reading labels, signs, warnings, etc.					
16. following schedules					
17. understanding announcements					
18. responding to job postings					
19. understanding memos					
20. giving and taking messages					

A. Pick your five most important goals. Copy them here.

The five goals I want to work on most are

1. _____

2. _____

3. _____

4. _____

5. _____

B. Think about these questions. Write your answers.

1. With whom do you need to speak better English at work?

_____

2. What do you need to talk about with that person?

_____

3. With whom would you like to speak better English at work?

_____

4. What would you like to talk about with that person?

_____

5. At work, what do you need to read or write about in English?

_____

6. What written materials at work would you like to understand and use better?

_____

UNIT 1

Communicating about a Job

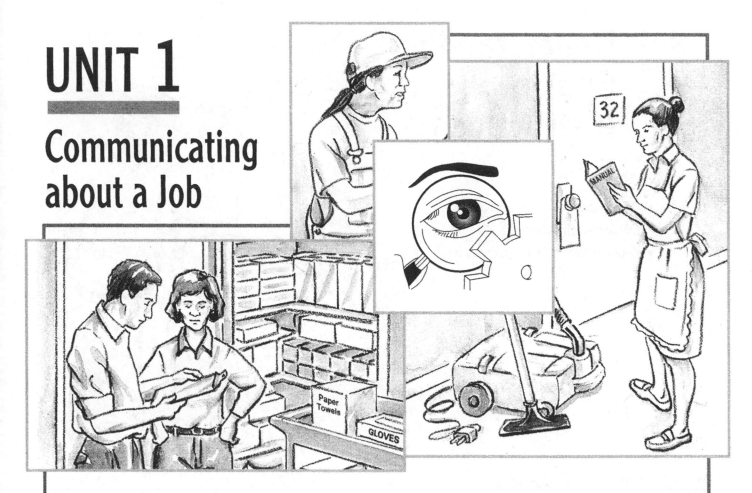

An important part of any job is using and sharing information about the work you do. Think about the ways you get new information about your work. Do you listen to others, or do you use written materials? Think about the ways in which you give information to others. Do you talk to them, or do you write things down?

In this unit, you will learn to communicate and use information about your job more effectively. You will practice

- listening to instructions
- giving instructions to other people
- following written instructions
- telling people about the work that you do
- keeping records of the work that you do

LESSON 1

Understanding Spoken Instructions

Objectives

- Understand spoken instructions
- Clarify meaning of instructions
- Get more information if you need it

Warm-Up

Talk about your experience.

- Name something you can do well.
- How did you learn to do it?

Talk about the picture.

- Who are these people?
- What do you think they are saying?

Key Words for Work

logbook

inspect

key in

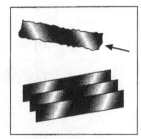

defective

Getting Instructions for a New Job

Sonia is getting instructions from her supervisor, Mike. She wants to make sure she understands everything that he tells her.

Mike: Sonia, you're going to cut the metal sheets that we use for our products.

Sonia: Sure, Mike. What do I need to do?

Mike: First, put a sheet of metal along the right edge of the cutting machine. Key in the size that you need. Then you can pull down the cutting blade.

When you're done, lift the blade. Then inspect each piece to make sure the edges are smooth. Put the finished pieces in your storage tray.

If a piece is defective, note that in the logbook.

Sonia: Let me see if I've got it. First, I take a sheet of metal and put it on the cutter. Where did you say it goes?

Mike: Along the right edge.

Sonia: OK. Then I key in the size and pull down the blade. When I finish, I lift the blade again, right?

Mike: Right. Then check to make sure all the edges are smooth.

Sonia: OK. And if the piece is all right, I put it in my storage tray. But what should I do if an edge is not smooth?

Mike: That's a defective piece. Put it in the red tray under your work-bench. And don't forget to write a note in your logbook.

Sonia: I won't. Well, I think I've got it now. Thanks, Mike.

Tips

Understanding Spoken Instructions
- Listen for the steps in a task.
- Picture yourself doing the task.
- Repeat the steps in your own words.
- Ask for more information if you need it.

Check Your Understanding

A. Review the Information

Check ✓ the correct answer.

1. What new job is Sonia learning?

   _____ **a.** how to lift the blade   _____ **c.** how to use a computer

   _____ **b.** how to use a logbook   _____ **d.** how to cut metal sheets

2. Which of these steps comes last?

   _____ **a.** pulling down the blade   _____ **c.** cutting a metal sheet

   _____ **b.** checking the edges   _____ **d.** lifting the blade

3. What does Sonia look for when she inspects each piece?

   _____ **a.** the size that she needs   _____ **c.** smooth edges

   _____ **b.** a note in the logbook   _____ **d.** the storage tray

4. Where should she put defective pieces?

   _____ **a.** in her storage tray   _____ **c.** on the cutting machine

   _____ **b.** in her red tray   _____ **d.** in her logbook

B. Discuss the Questions

1. Why does Sonia repeat Mike's instructions?

2. During the conversation on page 9, does Sonia remember everything Mike tells her? How do you know?

3. How do you think Sonia feels when she asks, "What should I do if an edge is not smooth?" How do you think Mike feels?

4. What information does Sonia have to write in the logbook? Why do you think this information is important?

5. Does Sonia think she can do this job? How do you know?

6. In what ways has Sonia used the Tips? Do you think they will help her do her job? Why or why not?

Asking Questions about a Job

What other questions could Sonia ask about Mike's instructions?
Use the key words and write questions about her job.

1. (Where/metal sheets) _____

2. (How/inspect) _____

3. (What/logbook) _____

4. (Why/logbook) _____

Another Way to Say It

Work with a partner or team. Look at what Sonia says to Mike.
Write other ways to say these things.

1. "Let me see if I've got it."

   Your idea: _____

2. "Where did you say it goes?"

   Your idea: _____

3. "When I finish, I lift the blade again, right?"

   Your idea: _____

4. "I think I've got it now."

   Your idea: _____

Try It Out

A. Work with a Partner to Give and Follow Instructions

Draw diagrams. Use these shapes: circle, triangle, square, diagonal line.

One partner reads aloud the instructions in Set 1. The second partner follows the instructions and draws a diagram. The partners can ask and answer any questions. Then change roles.

Set 1

Draw a triangle. Draw a circle inside it. Make an X under the circle. Draw a square on the triangle. Draw two circles in the square. Draw a diagonal line from one side of the square to the opposite side.

Set 2

Draw a circle. Draw a square around the circle. Draw a diagonal line across the square. Draw a triangle over the circle. Draw a circle around the triangle. Make an X in the circle.

B. Share Your Drawing with the Class

Are the drawings the same or different? What do you think caused your results?

As a group, try to rewrite the instructions so there is only one result for each set. Then try out the instructions on someone outside the class. Bring in the drawings. Compare your results with the class. Do all the drawings look the same now? What changes did you make in the instructions, and how did they change the results?

C. Discuss the Question

When people give or follow instructions at your workplace, do the results have to be identical? Why or why not?

Wrap-Up

A. Understanding Workplace Culture

Work with a partner or team. This sign is posted at Sonia's workplace, outside Mike's office. Read and discuss the sign. Make sure you understand what Mike is saying. Then discuss the questions.

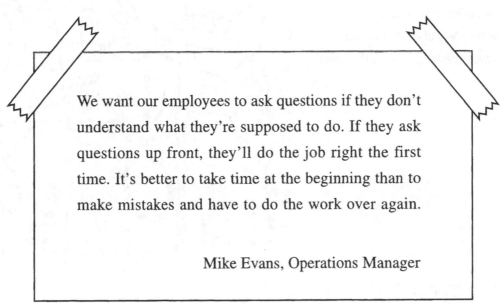

We want our employees to ask questions if they don't understand what they're supposed to do. If they ask questions up front, they'll do the job right the first time. It's better to take time at the beginning than to make mistakes and have to do the work over again.

Mike Evans, Operations Manager

1. Do you agree with Mike? Why or why not?

2. Is this the way that people think and behave at your workplace? How is it the same or different?

3. How do you feel about asking questions when someone gives you directions?

B. Application

Discuss the questions.

1. Who gives you instructions at your workplace? What tasks do they give you instructions for? Do you understand their instructions? What can you do if you don't understand?

2. Who do you give instructions to at work? What tasks do you give them instructions for? Do they often ask questions? What kinds of questions do they ask? Why do you think they ask those questions?

Giving Spoken Instructions

Objectives

- Give spoken instructions
- Put the steps of a task in order
- Answer questions about instructions

Warm-Up

Talk about your experience.

- When do you give instructions to people?
- What kinds of instructions do you give?

Talk about the picture.

- What are these people doing?
- Why do you think they are doing this?

Key Words for Work

power roller

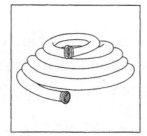
hose

connect

faucet

Giving Spoken Instructions

Wang is training to be a housepainter. Janet is giving Wang instructions about how to clean the hose of a power paint roller.

Janet: I see you've finished painting. Now you have to clean the hose on the power roller.

Wang: Can't it wait until tomorrow?

Janet: It has to be done as soon as you finish painting. Dry paint clogs the hose. Then the paint won't flow.

Wang: I understand. So what do I do first?

Janet: Before you do anything, turn the motor off. Let's see now. First put the end of the handle into the paint can. Then start the motor. This drains the paint from the hose. Next, connect the hose to the faucet. No, wait! Before you connect the hose, turn the motor off. Is that clear?

Wang: Not really. Is the motor off when I drain the paint?

Janet: No. You turn the motor on to drain the paint and off when you connect the hose to the faucet. Now, put the end of the handle in the sink. Turn on the cold water. When the water is clear, the hose is clean.

Wang: Is the motor off when the water is in the hose?

Janet: That's right. And last, you dry the hose and handle and put them in the box. Any questions?

Wang: I think I have it. Watch me and I'll try it.

Tips

Giving Spoken Instruction
- Think through the steps of the task.
- Explain the general reason for the task.
- Try to give the steps in sequence.
- Check that instructions are understood.

Check Your Understanding

A. Review the Information

Check ✓ **on** or **off**.

When Wang	the motor is	
	on	**off**
1. paints		
2. puts the handle in the paint can		
3. drains paint from the hose		
4. connects the hose to the faucet		
5. runs water through the hose		
6. wipes the hose and handle		

B. Discuss the Questions

1. What seem to be the most important steps that Janet wants Wang to remember?

2. Why did Janet have to say "Wait!" after she told Wang to connect the hose to the faucet?

3. How does Wang make sure he understands Janet's instructions?

4. How do Janet and Wang get along? Does Wang feel comfortable getting instructions from Janet? How do you know?

5. Which of the Tips for giving spoken instructions does Janet use? Do you think the Tips could help her give better instructions?

6. How does Janet convince Wang to clean his equipment right away? Why is it important to keep tools clean?

Using Sequence Words

Choose the correct sequence expression to complete each sentence.

1. _____, turn the motor off _____
   (First, Next)   (before, as soon as)

   you do anything.

2. _____, drain the paint into the paint can.
   (Last, Next)

3. _____, connect the hose to the faucet.
   (After that, Before that)

4. _____, wipe the tools and put them in the box.
   (Before that, Last)

Giving Clear Instructions

A. Put the Steps in Order

Pick a simple process (making a sandwich, changing a light-bulb) that you do at work or at home. Write each step of your instructions on a separate card or paper strip. Mix the order. Trade instructions with a partner. Put the partner's steps in order. Ask questions if necessary. Finally, have your partner check your work.

Then present the instructions to the rest of the class. Use sequence words so that the order of the steps is clear.

B. Using Tools

Work with a partner. Take turns describing how to take care of a tool used at work or at home. Give the steps in order, using sequence words. The other person will listen and ask questions.

Try It Out

Work with a partner. One of you will read Form A, "Changing Sandpaper in an Electric Sander." The other one will read Form B, "Draining Outdoor Faucets for Winter."

Read Form A or Form B silently. Make sure you understand all the words. Then you and your partner will take turns reading your instructions aloud. The other person will listen and take notes. You may answer each other's questions. Then your partner will tell you the steps in order from his or her notes. Correct the work together.

Form A

Changing Sandpaper in an Electric Sander

1. Turn off the sander.
2. Unplug the cord.
3. Raise the lever and remove old sandpaper.
4. Insert new sandpaper.
5. When sandpaper is in place, push the lever down.

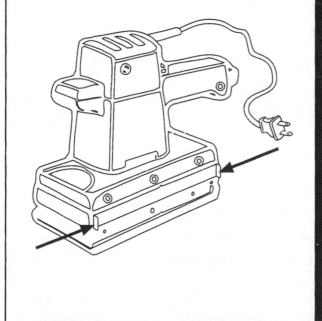

Form B

Draining Outdoor Faucets for Winter

1. Turn handle of the indoor feeder valve.
2. Open all outside faucets.
3. Unscrew the brass cap under the feeder valve.
4. Keep the brass cap open for 10 seconds to let out air.
5. Close the brass cap tightly.

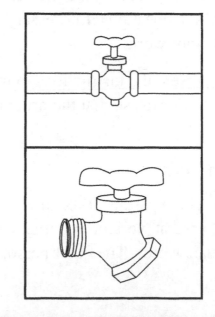

Wrap-Up

A. Understanding Workplace Culture

Work with a team. Talk about how you feel when you don't understand someone's directions.

Some people make it easy to ask questions. Others make it hard. Discuss what makes the two groups different.

Then brainstorm two lists. For List 1, write things people do or say that make it hard to ask questions when you don't understand.

> **For example:** People seem impatient.

For List 2, write things people do or say that make you feel it's OK to ask questions when you don't understand.

> **For example:** People ask if you are ready to try the task.

List 1	List 2
_____	_____
_____	_____
_____	_____
_____	_____

B. Application

Discuss the questions.

1. What kinds of tasks have you taught someone to do? Was that person successful? If the person had problems, what were they? How did you solve them?

2. What can you say to people who do things that are on List 1? How can you try to use List 2 when you have to give instructions to someone else?

LESSON 3 Using Written Instructions

Objectives

- Understand written instructions
- Scan for specific information
- Put the steps in written instructions in order

Warm-Up

Talk about your experience.

- What written instructions do you use at work? At home?
- Do the instructions you use have pictures or diagrams? If so, are they helpful? Why or why not?

Talk about the picture.

- What kind of workplace is this?
- What do you think the woman is doing?

Key Words for Work

vacuum cleaner

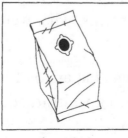
dust bag

power switch

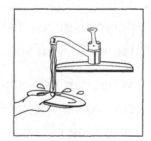
rinse

Using Written Instructions

Marta is a housekeeper in a large hotel. She vacuums the guest rooms and the hallways. Recently, she got a new vacuum cleaner. These are the instructions for changing the dust bag in the vacuum.

How to Change the Dust Bag

1. Turn off the power switch and unplug the electrical cord before changing the dust bag.

2. Lift the latch to remove the dust bag lid. Remove the used bag and dispose of it properly.

3. Clean the motor filter. Take the filter off and shake it to remove dust. Or rinse with warm water. Make sure the filter is completely dry before replacing it to prevent damage to the motor.

4. Unfold a new bag. Slide the bag shield into the track. Make sure the bag opening fully covers the air outlet.

5. Replace the dust bag lid. Fasten the latch securely.

Tips

Understanding Written Instructions
- Before you do anything, read all the instructions and look at diagrams or pictures.
- Do the steps in order as you reread the instructions.
- Check your work.

Check Your Understanding

A. Review the Information

Use the words in the box to complete the sentences.

replace	filter	latch	warm	power switch

1. Turn the _____ off before you change the bag.

2. Clean the _____ to keep dust out of the motor.

3. Use only _____ water to wash off the filter.

4. Dry the filter completely before you _____ it.

5. Put the lid on and close the _____ securely.

B. Discuss the Questions

1. Why is it important to turn off the power switch and unplug the cord before changing the dust bag? Have you seen this step in other instructions? If so, where?

2. How can diagrams and pictures help when you are following written instructions? Did the pictures on page 21 help you understand the instructions? Why or why not?

3. Look at the Tips for understanding written instructions. When you use written instructions, do you read all the steps first? Or do you start to follow the instructions right away? Does it make a difference?

4. If you follow the instructions on page 21 for changing a dust bag, how can you check your work?

5. Have you ever read instructions that were not clear? What did you do?

Follow the Steps in Order

Read the steps for changing the dust bag for a vacuum cleaner.
Number the steps in order.

_____ Clean the filter by shaking or rinsing it.

_____ Unfold the new dust bag.

_____ Put the full dust bag in the trash.

_____ Turn off the power switch.

_____ Fasten the latch on the dust bag lid.

_____ Replace the motor filter.

_____ Remove the full dust bag.

_____ Open the dust bag lid.

_____ Place the new dust bag over the air outlet.

Using Action Words

Use the words in the box to complete the sentences.

Rinse	Lift	Shake	Remove	Cover

1. _____ these boxes onto the top shelf.

2. _____ the boxes so that nothing will fall out.

3. _____ the tablecloth to get rid of the crumbs.

4. _____ the dishes from the table after dinner.

5. _____ the dishes in hot water.

Scanning Written Instructions

To scan for information, read very fast. Don't read all the words. Look only for the information you need.

Here are instructions for installing an air conditioner. Scan the paragraph for tools from the list. Check the tools you find.

Take air conditioner out of carton. Remove locking clips with a screwdriver. Slide unit out of cabinet. Measure width of the window with a tape measure. Cut sealing ribbon to that length with a sharp knife. Raise the bottom sash. Paste sealing ribbon along the bottom edge. Install cabinet in the window. Use a level to make sure it isn't tilted. Then slide the unit into the cabinet. Tap gently with a hammer until it snaps into place.

Tool List

_____ drill
_____ hammer
_____ knife
_____ level
_____ tape measure
_____ pliers
_____ saw
___✓___ screwdriver
_____ wrench

Try It Out

Work with a partner. Scan the yellow pages to look for a new heating system for your workplace. Take notes. Discuss the questions.

1. What category did you look under?

2. How many companies did you find?

3. Which one is closest to your job? Copy the name and phone

   number here. _____

Wrap-Up

A. Understanding Workplace Culture

Interview people in your class. Ask them if they use written
instructions at work or at home. Complete the chart. Compare
your results with the class.

Name/Country	At Work	At Home	Other
Diego/Peru	don't use	to make furniture; to fix things	to give directions to my house

B. Application

Bring in a set of written instructions that you use at work, that
you have used at home (how to install a smoke detector, make a
table, or program a VCR), or that you have copied (how to use
an ATM or a gas pump). Tell the class

- what the instructions are for

- the purpose of pictures or diagrams, if there are any

- how helpful the instructions are

- what problems you had with them, if you had any

- suggestions you would make if a friend was using the instructions

Describing Results

Objectives

- Describe completed work
- Give details about unfinished work
- Use quantity terms accurately

Warm-Up

Talk about your experience.

- What things about your work do you tell others when you finish your job for the day?
- What people do you tell, and why do you tell them?

Talk about the picture.

- What kind of workplace is this?
- What do you think the people are saying to each other?

Key Words for Work

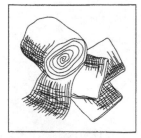
gauze bandages

rubber gloves

paper towels

supply cart

Describing Results

Albert and Lourdes work in a health clinic. They work in the stockroom. Albert just finished his shift. Lourdes is starting her shift. Albert is describing the work he finished and what he didn't finish.

Albert: Glad to see you, Lourdes. I'm ready to go home.

Lourdes: Hello, Albert. I'm ready to start. How far did you get today?

Albert: Here's the work order for this week. I checked off what I finished. Examining rooms 1 to 12 are all stocked. I started room 13, but I didn't finish it. So it's not checked off.

Lourdes: OK. Are we low on any supplies?

Albert: Yes. We need gauze bandages. The regular order came two days ago. But bandages go fast. Please order a gross of each size.

Lourdes: Gauze bandages, check. Do we need any rubber gloves?

Albert: I ordered gloves last week. I ordered alcohol wipes then, too. They should get here in a few days.

Lourdes: Good. And I saw six dozen packs of paper towels in the closet. Those will last for a while. So there are enough gloves, wipes, and towels. I'll order more bandages. And I'm ready to start at room 13. I see you filled my supply cart, too. Thanks.

Albert: No problem. I'll see you tomorrow, Lourdes.

```
┌─ Tips ─────────────────────────────────────────┐
│                                                 │
│   Describing Results                            │
│   • Tell what you finished.                     │
│   • Give details about the work you didn't      │
│     finish.                                     │
│   • Answer any questions about your work.       │
│                                                 │
└─────────────────────────────────────────────────┘
```

Check Your Understanding

A. Review the Information

Check ✓ **true** or **false**.

True	False	
_____	_____	1. Albert is leaving work now.
_____	_____	2. Lourdes finished rooms 1 to 12.
_____	_____	3. They need a total of one gross of gauze bandages.
_____	_____	4. Albert ordered rubber gloves last week.
_____	_____	5. Lourdes has to order alcohol wipes.
_____	_____	6. There are enough paper towels.
_____	_____	7. Room 13 is already stocked.
_____	_____	8. Lourdes has to stock her cart.

B. Discuss the Questions

1. How does Lourdes know what she has to do on her shift? What kinds of things does Albert tell her?

2. How did Albert know what to do on his shift?

3. How well do Albert and Lourdes get along? How do you know?

4. How well do you think Albert follows the Tips for describing results? Give examples that show him following the Tips.

5. Does Lourdes remember everything Albert tells her? How do you know?

Using Time Expressions

A. Complete the Sentences

Use the calendar to complete the sentences. Use a word or phrase from the box to describe each date. Today is March 16.

Sunday	Monday	Tuesday	Wednesday	Thursday	Friday	Saturday
4	5	6	7	8	9	10
11	12	13	14	15	**16** today	17
18	19	20	21	22	23	24

days ago	a few days ago	last	last week
tomorrow	yesterday	in a few days	next week

1. Lourdes was on vacation _____. (March 4–10)

2. Albert saw a movie _____ Sunday. (March 11)

3. Albert has a dentist appointment _____. (March 17)

4. Lourdes will have to order towels _____. (March 19)

5. Albert got the last order of towels _____. (March 12)

6. Lourdes was sick two _____. (March 14)

7. Albert ordered bandages _____. (March 15)

8. Lourdes will work a different shift _____. (March 19–23)

B. Describe Your Work

Use time expressions to write about your activities at work.

- yesterday
- next week
- a few days ago

- last week
- in a few days
- tomorrow

Try It Out

A. Asking Questions

Lourdes asks a lot of questions about the work she needs to do.
Write questions for her to ask in this conversation with Albert.

1. **Lourdes:** _____

   Albert: You'll have to start in room 5 tonight.

2. **Lourdes:** _____

   Albert: I filled all the paper towel dispensers already.

3. **Lourdes:** _____

   Albert: Please order five cartons of gloves. They get used up fast.

4. **Lourdes:** _____

   Albert: Yes, all of the rooms need clean glasses. And you'd better fill the soap
   dispensers, also.

B. Using Quantity Terms

Interview friends or co-workers. Ask them what kinds of things
come in the following quantities. Complete the chart. Then compare
your results with the class.

a bottle of	a carton of	a crate of
_____	_____	_____
_____	_____	_____
a dozen (12)	a gallon of	a liter of
_____	_____	_____
_____	_____	_____

Wrap-Up

A. Understanding Workplace Culture

Work with a team. Read this report. Discuss the questions.

> I am thrilled to report a major new account with the town of Wheeling. On July 1, Wheeling gave us 1,500 new medical insurance contracts. This brings our statewide tally up to 4,800 new contracts this year!
>
> Special thanks to Bunthan Tan and Fernanda Alvarez, whose outstanding work boosted the market share totals for the whole regional office.
>
> Ellen Martin
> VP, Municipal Markets Division

1. Does your company report to employees about special achievements, changes, or problems? Why do you think it does or does not inform employees?

2. Do you think that a company should describe its successes and failures to its employees? Why or why not?

B. Application

Interview some workers. Ask them who they tell about the results of their work. Find out what kinds of things they tell, and when they do it. Make a chart following the example below. Then compare your results with the class.

Name	Who to Tell	What to Tell	When to Tell
Sergio	his supervisor	machine problems; # assemblies completed	end of his shift

Documenting Results

Objectives

- Record completed work
- Read and understand charts
- Check records for accuracy
- Follow required formats for documentation

Monthly Stock Inventory Summary		
Stock Number/ Item	Delivered	Back Ordered
EP5 elbow pipe	240 gross	-0-
FT79 flexible tubing	980 ft.	500 ft.
HS76 hacksaw	27	24
TP32 1-ft. pipes	60 dozen	-0-
PW04 pipe wrench	6 special orders	-0-

Warm-Up

Talk about your experience.

- Do you have to keep records at your job? If so, what records do you keep and why?
- Do you keep any records at home? If so, why?

Talk about the chart.

- What information can you get from this chart?
- Why do companies use charts like this?

Key Words for Work

delivery man

elbow pipe

shower head

pipe wrench

Documenting Results

Raul Delgado is a delivery man for Paskin Plumbing Supply. He spends six hours a day making deliveries. Raul has to keep a record of the deliveries he makes. This is his record sheet for June 10.

Contact Name/ Company/ Address	Stock Number/ Item Name	Quantity	Date Rec'd/ Rec'd By/ Time
Paula Santos Santos Inc. 33 West St. urgent	EP5 elbow pipe SH09 shower heads	✓ 6 gross 8 gross ✓ 2 gross	6/10 PS 10:50 am
Sid Melrose Omar & Melrose 77 E. Bayville Rd. Special order	TP32 1-ft. pipes SH09 shower heads HS76 hacksaw	✓ 4 dozen ✓ 1 gross BO 2	6/10 back order ASAP
Warren James James Plumbing 606 First Ave. deliver to 90 Parker, side street	EP5 elbow pipe FT 79 flexible tubing PW04 pipe wrench	✓ 1 gross 5 gross ✓ 150 feet ✓ 2	WPJ 2:30 p.m.
Li Chu WJC Plumbers 95 Parker St. Special Order	FT 79 flexible tubing EP5 elbow pipe PW04 pipe wrench	✓ 200 feet BO 2 gross next day ✓ 1	6/10 2:50 p.m. 6/10

Tips

Documenting Results
- Record names and numbers accurately.
- Make sure information is complete.
- Check information in records. Correct any errors.
- Maintain records in proper format.

Check Your Understanding

A. Review the Information

Check ✓ the correct names. You may check more than one name.

Raul	Santos	Melrose	James	Chu
1. made a morning delivery to				
2. delivered extra elbow pipes to				
3. had back orders for				
4. delivered shower heads to				
5. went to Parker Street for				
6. had a special order for				
7. forgot to get initials from				
8. took pipe wrenches to				

B. Discuss the Questions

1. Do you think that Raul keeps careful records of his deliveries? Why or why not?

2. Why does Raul sometimes writes *BO* (for *back order*) on his delivery record? What will he do with this information?

3. Does Raul check the accuracy of the information in his records? How do you know?

4. Who do you think uses the special notes *(urgent, special order)* that he puts down for some customers?

5. What parts of the record sheet does Raul fill in carefully? What does he need to work on?

6. What other people or departments probably use the information Raul puts on his daily record sheets? What do you think they use the information for?

Finding and Using Details

A. What Do the Headings Mean?

Look at the top line of Raul's delivery record. He puts special information under each heading. Match each heading to the question that it answers.

Column Heading	Question
_____ 1. Contact Name/Company	a. What was delivered?
_____ 2. Stock Number/Item Name	b. When was the delivery made?
_____ 3. Address	c. Who gets the delivery?
_____ 4. Quantity	d. Where was the delivery made?
_____ 5. Date Rec'd	e. How much product was delivered?

B. Figure Mileage and Cost

1. Raul has to keep a tally of the miles he drives on his shift each week. Do the math to complete the chart.

MILEAGE SUMMARY FOR TRUCK #35, SHIFT 1

week of: ___March 23___

Day	Start	End	Total
Monday	22,698	22,851	
Tuesday	22,897	23,044	
Wednesday	23,044	23,290	
Thursday	23,321	23,499	
Friday	23,607	23,692	
		Total:	

signed: Raul Delgado

2. It costs $.22 a mile to use this truck. How much did the truck cost during Shift 1 this week? $_____

Try It Out

Work with a partner. Read and discuss the chart. Look at the headings. List the places where you think information is missing.

Company/Town/ Contact Name	Stock #/Item	Quantity	Date Promised
Joe Mill	TP32 - pipe SH09 shower heads	9 gross 2 gross	
BathCo Bayville	EL elbow pipe	90 feet	6/18
Ray Ferris	PW04 pipe wrench	5	*special order*
Acme Inc./Barre Esther		6 gross	6/18

_____

_____

_____

_____

_____

_____

Then one partner takes Role A, and the other takes Role B. Give each person a name. Create a conversation. Present it to the class.

Role A

You are a salesperson. This is part of your weekly record. Talk about the problems you have keeping complete records.

Role B

You are a supervisor. Talk about why accurate records are important. Suggest things the salesperson can do to improve.

Wrap-Up

A. Understanding Workplace Culture

In this country, almost everyone who works uses written documents. Interview some workers. Ask them what kinds of results they document at their job. Find out how they report the results. Find out why these documents are important. Complete the chart.

Name/Job	What	How	Why
Jan/sells shoes	each sale has a slip	sales slips are tallied every week; results put on a graph	gets commission; store knows popular shoe brands

B. Application

Work with a team. Discuss the interviews you conducted. Compare your results with the team. Discuss the questions.

1. What documents do most people know of or use?

2. What are the most common reasons for documenting results? Which do you think are the most important?

With your team, report to the class on what you learned about documenting results.

UNIT 1 REVIEW

Many things that you hear or read at work use informal expressions, special workplace terms, or idioms. Rewrite these statements and questions based on Unit 1. Use more formal language.

1. I want you to ask questions up front.

_____

2. Check that the edges are smooth.

_____

3. I checked off what I finished.

_____

4. Bandages go fast.

_____

5. Note that in your logbook.

_____

6. Is that clear?

_____

7. How far did you get today?

_____

8. I think I have it.

_____

UNIT 2
Following Safety Procedures

Safety in the workplace is one of the highest priorities for both workers and companies. Often, workplace safety simply means following basic rules or procedures. And at times those procedures can prevent injury or death. Think about safety procedures you follow at work or at home. Do you use any special clothing or gear? Do you follow any special signs, warnings, or rules to make sure you are doing things safely?

In this unit, you will expand your understanding of safety at work. You will learn about
- basic safety gear
- common safety rules and regulations
- the importance of following safety rules
- ways to deal with safety problems

LESSON 6 Using Safety Gear

Objectives

- Identify basic safety gear
- Learn why safety gear is necessary
- Understand why safety gear must be kept in good condition

Warm-Up

Talk about your experience.

- Do you wear any special clothing for safety at work? At home? If so, why do you wear it?
- Who decides what special clothing or safety gear you wear at work?

Talk about the picture.

- What parts of the body are protected by the safety gear in the picture?

Key Words for Work

hairnet

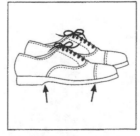
rubber soles

blender

hard hat

Using Special Safety Gear

Rosa and Leon clean industrial fabrics. They wash the fabrics with liquid chemicals. Sometimes liquid spills on the floor. That's why they have to wear shoes with rubber soles at work.

Rosa: I don't like wearing these shoes. They're ugly.

Leon: They're not so bad. The rubber soles keep you from slipping on a wet floor. They keep your feet dry, too.

Rosa: I know. But I want to wear my nice shoes sometimes.

Leon: Don't feel so bad. My daughter has to wear a hairnet at her job. She doesn't like it, but she's a cook.

Rosa: Hairnets don't look good, but they do keep hair out of the food.

Leon: With a hairnet, her hair won't catch on fire from the stove. And it won't get caught in the blenders and mixers she uses.

Rosa: I never thought of that. I guess most people need special gear at work. My son is a medical aide. He has to wear rubber gloves when he works with blood. The gloves protect him from diseases. And my husband always wears a hard hat at construction sites.

Leon: Of course. That's an OSHA rule.

Rosa: What's OSHA?

Leon: It's a government agency. It's the Occupational Safety and Health Administration. OSHA makes rules to protect workers.

Tips

Protecting Yourself with Safety Gear
- Find out what safety gear is required for your job.
- Understand why the safety gear is used.
- Find out how to get the safety gear that you need.
- Always use the required gear on the job.

Check Your Understanding

A. Review the Information

Match the safety gear to the worker who uses it.

_____ 1. rubber-soled shoes   **a.** a medical aide

_____ 2. rubber gloves   **b.** a construction worker

_____ 3. a hairnet   **c.** an industrial fabric cleaner

_____ 4. a hard hat   **d.** a cook

B. Discuss the Questions

1. Look at the safety gear and the workers in part A. What other protective gear do you think those workers use?

2. What other kinds of safety gear do you use or know about? How do those items protect workers?

3. What would you do if your safety gear was ugly? What would you do if it made you feel uncomfortable?

4. Rosa says, "I guess most people need special gear at work." Do you agree or disagree? Give examples that support your point of view.

5. How do Rosa and Leon get along? How can you tell? Do you and your co-workers ever talk about your families at work? How do you feel about that?

6. What does Leon mean when he says OSHA makes rules to protect workers?

7. Which Tips for protecting yourself with safety gear do Rosa and Leon follow? What do they do to follow those tips?

Categorizing

Use the words in the box to finish the chart. Each row should have a piece of gear, the body part it protects, and the hazard it protects against.

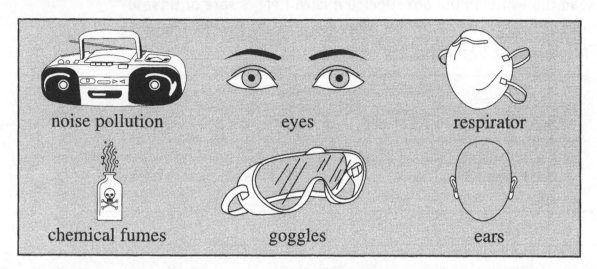

| noise pollution | eyes | respirator |
| chemical fumes | goggles | ears |

Gear	Body Part	Hazard
_____	_____	flying sparks
headphones	_____	_____
_____	lungs	_____

Try It Out

A. Safe or Unsafe?

Read the words in the box. Decide if each item is **safe** or **unsafe** to wear near machines. Write your answer under the right heading. Then add your own items.

work gloves	hard hats	goggles	loose sleeves
long hair	bracelets	hairnets	dangling earrings

Safe near Machines   **Unsafe near Machines**

_____   _____

_____   _____

_____   _____

_____   _____

_____   _____

B. Write about Safety

1. Work with a partner or team. Write a letter to a safety committee or union. Describe a workplace safety problem you know about. Tell why it is a problem. Use one of these ideas or one of your own:

    • There is not enough safety gear for every worker.
    • People do not clean up spills right away.
    • Everyone has a headache from the noise.

2. Trade letters with another team. Write an answer to the problem. Then share both letters with the class.

Wrap-Up

A. Understanding Workplace Culture

Read the workplace sign. Then discuss the questions.

SAFETY FIRST

✓ Inspect your safety gear!

✓ Repair your safety gear!

✓ Wear your safety gear!

1. Why is it important to take care of your safety gear? What could happen if your gear isn't in good condition?

2. What do you do if your safety gear is damaged? What happens if you forget your gear? What if there is not enough safety equipment for everyone?

3. Do you share your safety gear with others? Why or why not?

B. Application

Interview two or three workers. Ask them what safety gear they use at work, and why. Take notes and create a chart, following the example below. Compare your results with the class.

Job	Safety Gear	Reason
fabric cutter in factory	dust mask, apron	protect lungs and clothing

Understanding Rules and Regulations

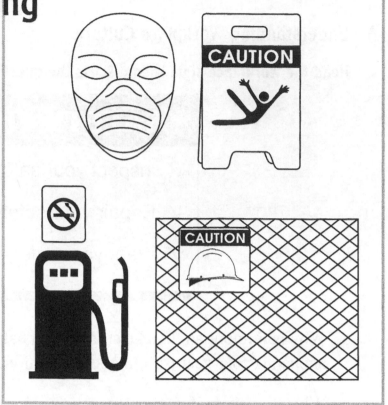

Objectives

- Understand safety rules and guidelines
- Learn the reasons for safety rules
- Learn regulations that help prevent accidents and injuries

Warm-Up

Talk about your experience.

- What safety rules do you have at work? At home?
- Who decides which safety rules are needed?

Talk about the picture.

- What rules do the signs in the picture tell you?
- Think about signs like these at your job. What rules do those signs tell you?

Key Words for Work

first-aid kit

alarm pull

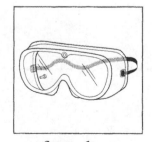

safety glasses

extinguisher

Working Safety

Sanders Industries follows the safety regulations of OSHA. OSHA is a government agency. It makes rules and guidelines to protect workers' safety and health.

SAFETY AT SANDERS INDUSTRIES

Emergency Exits Keep all exits clear. Keep doors unlocked. Do not place boxes or trash in front of doors.

Protective Gear All workers must wear earplugs and safety glasses on the manufacturing floor. Your supervisors will hand out protective gear at the start of each shift. Workers must put on protective items before turning on machines.

Medical and First Aid There is a complete emergency first-aid kit for every 25 workers next to the main stairway on all floors.

Fire Protection There are fire extinguishers and alarm pulls at every exit and in the lunchroom. There is absolutely NO SMOKING on the manufacturing floors.

Tips

Understanding Safety Rules and Regulations
- Discuss safety policies with your supervisor.
- Identify and locate safety equipment in your work area.
- Find out how to get safety gear that you need on the job.
- Ask questions. Make sure you understand safety rules.

Check Your Understanding

A. Review the Details

Check ✓ the correct sentence.

1. _____ **a.** The company gives out protective gear.

   _____ **b.** Workers buy their own protective gear.

2. _____ **a.** There are fire extinguishers at each workstation.

   _____ **b.** There are fire extinguishers at each exit.

3. _____ **a.** Keep exit doors locked to keep out strangers.

   _____ **b.** Keep exit doors unlocked and clear for emergencies.

4. _____ **a.** First-aid kits are located on all floors.

   _____ **b.** First-aid kits are located in the head office.

5. _____ **a.** Workers cannot smoke on the manufacturing floors.

   _____ **b.** Workers cannot smoke anywhere at Sanders Industries.

6. _____ **a.** Workers put on safety gear before they turn on their machines.

   _____ **b.** Workers turn on their machines before they put on safety gear.

B. Discuss the Questions

1. Do you know where the emergency exits are at your job? At your school? Where else have you seen emergency exits?

2. Why do you think there is no smoking on the manufacturing floors at Sanders Industries? What is the smoking policy at your job?

3. How did you learn the safety rules at your job? Who can you ask if you have questions about the safety rules?

4. How do the safety rules at your job compare to those at Sanders Industries? How are they similar or different?

Safety Rules and Reasons

List A lists some common safety rules and guidelines. List B lists reasons for following those safety rules. Match each rule in List A to its reason in List B. Then write two safety rules of your own, with the reasons for those rules.

List A: Safety Rules

_____ 1. Don't leave tools or trash on the floor.

_____ 2. Wear rubber-soled shoes on the shop floor.

_____ 3. Don't pull plugs out by the cord.

_____ 4. Wear earplugs when machinery is turned on.

_____ 5. Keep the lid on all chemicals that are not in use.

_____ 6. Don't breathe in the fumes from chemicals.

_____ 7. _____

_____

_____ 8. _____

_____

List B: Safety Reasons

a. to prevent getting a shock

b. to make sure no one trips or falls

c. to protect your hearing

d. to prevent getting sick or poisoned

e. to make sure you don't slip on wet floors

f. to prevent spilling dangerous liquids

g. _____

_____

h. _____

_____

Talking about Safety Rules and Reasons

Work with a partner. Take turns asking and answering questions about the rules and reasons.

For example: • Why can't I leave my tools on the floor?
• How can I protect my hearing?

Try It Out

A. What Rule Was Broken?

In each picture, safety rules are being broken. Read the rules on the sign from Sanders Industries. Match each picture to the rules being broken.

SAFETY RULES FOR SANDERS INDUSTRIES

   a. Keep all emergency exits clear and unlocked.

   b. Report damaged equipment right away.

   c. Wear safety glasses around machines.

   d. Wear hard hats on the factory floor.

   e. Clean up all spills right away.

   f. There is NO SMOKING in the factory.

1.

2.

B. Talk about Safety

Work with a partner or team. Describe each picture in part A. Tell what the workers are doing. Then tell what they should or should not do to follow the safety rules. Finally, tell why it is important for the workers to follow the safety rules.

Wrap-Up

A. Understanding Workplace Culture

Work with a partner or team. Read the information about work injuries. Then discuss the questions.

Common Work Injuries

A repetitive-motion injury comes from doing the same motion many, many times over. Typists, assembly workers, and data processors can get this kind of injury. Change your position frequently and relax your wrist to lower your risk of this kind of injury.

Back injuries are very common. All workers, from furniture movers to waitresses, can hurt their backs. But you can lower your risk. For example, push handcarts; don't pull them. Squat to lift things from the floor; don't bend at the waist.

---

1. What other types of workers can get these injuries?

2. What other things can you do to prevent these injuries?

3. Why is preventing injuries and accidents important to businesses? How can injuries or accidents cost businesses money?

B. Application

Look for safety signs at your job or around your neighborhood. Copy the signs and write down where you saw each one. Discuss with the class what each sign means and why it was in the place where you saw it. Where else can you see those signs?

LESSON 8 Following Safety Rules

Objectives

- Understand reasons for following safety rules
- Understand verbal warnings
- Understand warning signs

Warm-Up

Talk about your experience.

- What safety warnings have you given at work? At home?
- What safety warnings have you heard?

Talk about the picture.

- What do you think is happening in this picture?
- Who are these people?

Key Words for Work

face shield

table saw

hinge

hand sanding

Following Safety Rules

Lia works for Tip Top Furniture Designs. She works with a table saw. She has to wear special safety gear. Today Jaya, her supervisor, is warning her about using the wrong equipment.

Jaya: Lia, where's your face shield? The rules say you have to wear a shield at the table saw.

Lia: I know. But the hinge broke yesterday. I forgot to get it fixed. I have my goggles, though. So my eyes are protected.

Jaya: I'm sorry. You can't use the table saw without a face shield.

Lia: But I'll lose a lot of time if I get it fixed now. It's not very comfortable anyway. It's not that important.

Jaya: It's very important. Dust and splinters are always flying around the table saw. You could be hurt.

Lia: But that hardly ever happens!

Jaya: It only takes one time for a serious injury. And if you aren't wearing the right gear, then Tip Top is liable. That means we are responsible, not the insurance company.

Lia: All right. I see your point. But what should I do?

Jaya: Fix the face shield right after work. For now, I'll put you on a job that doesn't require the face shield—like hand sanding. But if it isn't fixed tomorrow, you'll have to take time off.

Lia: Hand sanding? Isn't there anything else to do?

Tips

Following Safety Rules
- Always use the proper safety gear.
- Don't use alternative equipment without permission.
- Understand the reasons for using safety gear.
- Repair or replace damaged equipment right away.

Check Your Understanding

A. Review the Information

Check ✓ **true, false,** or **NI** (no information).

True	False	NI	
_____	_____	_____	1. Lia doesn't work without proper safety gear.
_____	_____	_____	2. Lia is Tip Top's best worker.
_____	_____	_____	3. Lia is responsible for her own safety gear.
_____	_____	_____	4. Lia knows how to do more than one job.
_____	_____	_____	5. Lia wants to do hand sanding.
_____	_____	_____	6. Jaya doesn't care if Lia uses goggles.
_____	_____	_____	7. Jaya worries about accidents on the job.
_____	_____	_____	8. Jaya tells Lia to buy a new face shield.

B. Discuss the Questions

1. Why doesn't Lia want to stop working on the table saw?

2. Does Lia feel she can disagree with Jaya? How can you tell? How well do you think they get along?

3. Lia wasn't happy with Jaya's solution. Was it a fair solution? Why or why not? What would you do if you were Lia's supervisor?

4. Do you think Jaya is a good or a bad supervisor? Give reasons to support your answer.

5. Which of the Tips for following safety rules does Lia *not* follow? What are her reasons for not following them?

6. What reasons does Jaya give Lia for using a face shield? Do you think Jaya's reasons are good? Why or why not?

Giving and Understanding Warnings

A. Look at the Safety Signs

Write a sentence that tells what to do or not to do when you see each sign.

1.

Don't _____

_____

3.

_____

_____

2.

_____

_____

4.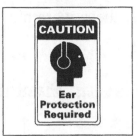

_____

_____

B. Make a Safety Sign for Work or School

Work with a partner. The sign can be serious or funny. Here are two examples.

Don't add water.

Wet Paint

Shout It Out!

Work with a partner or team. Here are some warnings you may hear at work. Make sure you understand each warning. Write a sentence that tells what to do when you hear the warning. Then discuss when and where you may hear these warnings.

1. Coming through!

Move out of the way. Let the other person pass.

2. Heads up!

_____

3. Duck!

_____

4. Look out!

_____

Try It Out

Look at the picture. How can workers prevent these problems?
Write some safety rules for these people to follow.

Safety Rules

_____

_____

_____

_____

Wrap-Up

A. Understanding Workplace Culture

In the conversation between Lia and her supervisor, Jaya states why Lia must follow workplace safety rules. Write her reasons. Then discuss the questions.

_____

_____

_____

1. Do you think Jaya's reasons are good ones? Why or why not? Which reason do you think is most important?

2. Do you think Jaya was too hard or too easy on Lia? Give reasons for your answer.

3. Would you talk to your supervisor the way Lia talked to Jaya? Why or why not? If not, what would you say to Jaya in this situation?

B. Application

1. Bring in or copy warning labels from items you have at home or at work (children's toys or equipment, medicine bottles, cleaning products, etc.). Read each label to the class, and explain why the item has that particular warning. Then rewrite the information from the labels in your own words.

2. What types of information do you normally find on warning labels? Make a class list. Discuss why each type is important.

LESSON 9

Safety Problems at Work

Objectives

- Know who to report problems to
- Understand that reporting problems is good for workers and companies
- Know what to do in an emergency

Warm-Up

Talk about your experience.

- What happens if someone is hurt at your workplace?
- Who do you tell when there is an accident or injury?

Talk about the picture.

- What do you think will happen to this man?
- Do you think he is careless? Why or why not?

Key Words for Work

warning sign

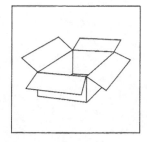

carton

slipped

Reporting an Accident

Jaime slipped on a wet floor at work. Subra saw the accident. Now Subra is talking to Irina, the building manager.

Irina: I'm glad you reported Jaime's accident fast. His boss is taking him to the hospital. Now I have to fill out an accident report.

Subra: An accident report? That sounds serious. Will I get in trouble? What about Jaime? Will he get in trouble?

Irina: Don't worry. It's important to get all the facts. Nothing will happen to you or Jaime. Can you tell me what you saw?

Subra: Well, OK. Jaime was carrying some big cartons. He slipped on the wet floor. There was a yellow warning sign. But Jaime couldn't see it. He was carrying too many cartons.

Irina: Carrying too many cartons. Then what happened?

Subra: I yelled to Jaime to watch out. But it was too late. He slipped on the wet floor! He went down! He was yelling in pain!

Irina: Could you tell why he was yelling?

Subra: He fell on his arm. Then the cartons fell on him. I tried to help him up. That made him yell louder. So I got you.

Irina: Poor Jaime. So he didn't see the sign, and he fell on his arm.

Subra: That's right. It happened so fast. Will Jaime be OK?

Irina: I'm sure he will. I'm going to write up this report now. Let me know if you remember anything else.

Tips

Dealing with Safety Problems or Accidents at Work
- Report unsafe conditions right away.
- Report accidents right away.
- Don't move injured people yourself.
- Be ready to describe what you saw.

Check Your Understanding

A. Review the Information

Check ✓ **true, false,** or **NI** (no information).

True	False	NI	
_____	_____	_____	1. Subra saw the warning sign.
_____	_____	_____	2. Jaime saw the warning sign.
_____	_____	_____	3. Jaime was late for work.
_____	_____	_____	4. Irina saw the accident.
_____	_____	_____	5. Subra called an ambulance.
_____	_____	_____	6. The cartons were heavy.
_____	_____	_____	7. Irina will write the report.
_____	_____	_____	8. Jaime broke his arm.

B. Discuss the Questions

1. How does Subra feel about telling Irina about the accident? How would you feel?

2. Do you think Subra or Jaime will get in trouble for the accident? Why or why not?

3. Why does Irina have to fill out an accident report?

4. Why did Subra get Irina after Jaime fell? Which tip on page 59 was he following? Why is this tip important?

5. How well do you think Irina gets along with Subra and Jaime? How well do you think Subra and Jaime get along?

6. Subra said Jaime couldn't see the warning sign because "he was carrying too many cartons." What would you do if you thought an accident was a co-worker's fault? How could an accident like this one be prevented?

Adding Important Facts

Subra remembered more details about the accident. Check ✓ the
details you think he should tell Irina. Compare your results with
the class.

_____ **1.** The accident happened after lunch.

_____ **2.** The cleaners often forget to put up the warning sign.

_____ **3.** Another worker almost fell, too. The warning sign was pushed
against the wall.

_____ **4.** Jaime is a new employee.

_____ **5.** A carton hit Jaime on the head. He had a small cut.

_____ **6.** Jaime was carrying three cartons.

_____ **7.** Jaime was on his way to the storeroom.

Understanding Warning Signs

Look at these warning signs. Write what each sign means. Then write
what you can say to warn a co-worker who does not see the sign.
Compare your ideas with the class.

Wet Floor _____ _____ _____

Watch out! The _____ _____ _____

floor is wet. _____ _____ _____

Try It Out

A. Filling Out an Accident Report

Irina has to fill out a report on Jaime's accident. Complete the
form. Use information from the conversation on page 59 and from
Subra's list on page 61.

**METRO INDUSTRIES, INC.
ACCIDENT REPORT**

Name of injured person: _____

Date of accident: ___*October 9, 2000*_____

Cause of accident: _____

_____

Describe injury (injuries): _____

Witness(es): _____

Name and position of person completing report:

_____

B. Asking for More Information

What other information do you think Irina needs for the
accident report? Make a list of questions she can ask to get
that information.

For example: What time did the accident take place?

Wrap-Up

A. Understanding Workplace Culture

Interview a friend who is working. Ask what happens if a worker
gets hurt on the job at the friend's workplace. Take notes below.
Compare information with the class.

Company name: _____

Who to tell about injury/accident: _____

Who files report: _____

Who decides when worker can return to job: _____

B. Application

Work in three teams. Team 1 will represent Jaime. Team 2 will
represent Irina. Team 3 will be mediators. Jaime's and Irina's
teams must defend their positions. The mediators will ask
questions and then decide when Jaime should go back to work.

Jaime says:
My supervisor told me to take some
cartons to the storeroom. He said,
"Come back quick. There's a lot of
work today." The cartons were empty,
so I carried them all together. I fell in
the hallway. No one told me the floor
was wet. I couldn't see a sign. Now I
hurt my arm. The doctor says I should
be out of work for two weeks.

Irina says:
The cleaning company's sign was in the
hallway. But Jaime was carrying too
many cartons. He couldn't see where
he was going. A doctor took X rays at
the hospital. The cartons didn't hurt
him much. His arm isn't broken. He
can do some kind of work here until
his arm is better.

UNIT 2 REVIEW

Change these incorrect workplace rules. Write rules that say what workers should do. Use information from Unit 2 or rules from your own workplace.

1. Wear safety gear only if it looks good on you.

   _____

2. You can't prevent back injuries, so don't even try.

   _____

3. If liquids spill, wait until the cleaners come at night.

   _____

4. Don't use safety gear that feels uncomfortable.

   _____

5. Report accidents at the end of your shift.

   _____

6. Keep exit doors locked at all times to keep out strangers.

   _____

7. If your gear breaks, fix it whenever you have a chance.

   _____

8. Carry as much as you can, to get your work done quickly.

   _____

UNIT 3

Working with Others

This unit examines the ways we work together with other people
- as co-workers
- as employees and supervisors
- as leaders and team members
- in companies and groups

Think about the different roles and relationships that people have at your workplace. Think about how easy or difficult it is for people to get along and to work together effectively.

In this unit you will practice skills that will help in working well with other people. You will learn how to
- understand workplace roles and responsibilities
- ask for and offer help
- express your opinion
- give and receive feedback about a job

LESSON 10 Understanding Roles and Responsibilities

Objectives

- Understand teamwork
- Recognize leadership qualities
- Learn how work decisions are made

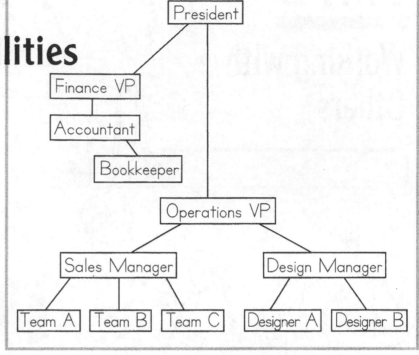

Warm-Up

Talk about your experience.

- Who do you report to at work? Who does that person report to?
- Who makes decisions about your work tasks?

Talk about the chart.

- What position on the chart is your job closest to now?
- Where would you like to be in five years? In 10 years?

Key Words for Work

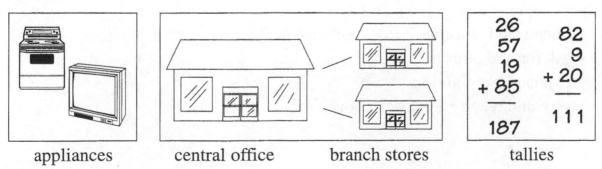

appliances   central office   branch stores   tallies

Knowing Who to Tell

Rudy works at a branch store of JMP Appliance Company. Mr. Ford, the store manager, discusses incomplete paperwork with Rudy. Then Rudy talks to his team leader, Greta, about the problem.

Mr. Ford: Rudy, I send the sales data for each team to the central office every Tuesday morning. But today Greta said your tallies weren't in your team's folder.

Rudy: I'm sorry they were late, sir. But I told your secretary I couldn't stay yesterday to finish my tallies. I had to pick up my children after work. I'll finish them up right now.

Mr. Ford: Too late. I already sent in the report. Your team's tallies were incomplete. Next time talk to Greta, not my secretary.

Rudy: I'm sorry, Mr. Ford. It won't happen again.

Later that day, Rudy told Greta what happened.

Greta: It's lucky the central office takes corrections late. Next time, report problems to me first. Oh! Did you hear? Cathy Blaine is the new assistant manager at the Stone Mall store.

Rudy: No kidding! How did that happen, Greta?

Greta: Cathy took JMP's training course for managers. She did very well, and the Stone Mall team asked her to apply. She just started working there.

Rudy: I'm happy for her. Maybe I should find out more about JMP's training courses.

Tips

Working in Teams
- Understand how your job fits in with others' jobs.
- Learn who to report to with problems or changes.
- Learn who depends on you for information or material.
- Learn who is responsible for making decisions.

Check Your Understanding

A. Review the Information

Use the words in the box to complete the summary.

branch store	leader	sales data
central office	manager	tallies

Greta is Rudy's team _____. She collects her team's

_____ for Mr. Ford. He is the _____ of

the _____. Each week he reports the

_____ for his store to the _____.

B. Discuss the Questions

1. Look at the Tips for working in teams. Which tip does Rudy not follow? What advice would you give him?

2. Do you think Rudy will get in trouble because he didn't turn in his tallies on time? Why or why not?

3. Do you think his reason for the late tallies was a good one? What would you do in Rudy's situation?

4. Do you think JMP Appliance Company might be a good place to work? Why or why not?

5. Does Rudy talk the same way to Mr. Ford as he does to Greta? What similarities or differences are there?

Using Two-Word Verbs

Find a two-word verb in the box that means the same as the
underlined verb in each sentence. Write the two-word verb in
the blank.

| find out | finish up | send in | pick up | try out |

_____ 1. The central office wants to <u>test</u> a new product.

_____ 2. I'll <u>get</u> a sample of the new product tomorrow.

_____ 3. I have to <u>learn</u> how well the new product works.

_____ 4. I'll <u>complete</u> my report for them soon.

_____ 5. Then I'll <u>mail</u> the report to Data Control.

What Makes a Good Leader?

Write a list of words or phrases that describe leaders. Decide if each
word or phrase describes an effective leader or a poor leader. List
them in the chart below. Then compare your results with the class.

Effective Leader	Poor Leader
gives helpful instructions	gives confusing instructions

Try It Out

A. Talking to a Co-worker

Work with a partner. One partner takes Role A, and the other takes Role B. Give each person a name. Create a conversation between the co-workers. Use ideas from the stories below, and make up new details. Discuss how to handle emergencies better in the future.

Role A

You work in a store with another member of your selling team (Role B). But yesterday, your partner never came to work. You missed your break time. Customers were angry about long lines. Finally, at lunch, your supervisor said a part-time sales-person would help you the rest of the day. Tell your teammate how you feel.

Role B

You work in a store with another member of your selling team (Role A). But yesterday, before work, you got a call from the hospital. Your child had fallen off a swing at school and was hurt. You went to the hospital and spent the day there. You called the store. The operator said she would give your message to the supervisor. Tell your teammate what happened.

B. Talking to a Supervisor

With your partner, work with another pair of students. The first pair will play the supervisor. The second pair will play the co-workers. They will present the conversation developed in Part A. They will ask how the supervisor felt about the situation yesterday. They will ask how they can prevent problems like this in the future.

C. Evaluate the Conversations in Part A and Part B

How well did you and your teammate get along? Were you able to find a solution for dealing with emergencies? How well did you each get along with your supervisor? What leadership qualities did your supervisor show?

Wrap-Up

A. Understanding Workplace Culture

Interview two or three classmates. Find out what their boss or supervisor is like. Ask what they would do differently or the same if they were a supervisor. Complete the chart. Compare your results with a team.

Name/Job	I Work In a Team	By Myself	My supervisor is . . .	If I were a supervisor . . .
Pritiben/ hotel maid	✓		very strict but treats everyone the same	I would listen to workers more. They know the problems on the floors. They have good ways to improve things. My boss doesn't listen to new ways.

B. Application

Look at the company chart on page 66. Make a chart of the job positions in your workplace. Start with your own job. Who do you work with? Who do you report to? Who reports to you? Try to find out who your supervisor reports to. If there are other positions in the company, put them on the chart.

Asking for and Offering Help

Objectives

- Understand who to ask for help and when
- Learn how to ask for help quickly and clearly
- Understand when and how to offer help
- Learn how to respond to requests for help

Warm-Up

Talk about your experience.

- How do you feel when you have to ask for help at work?
- What do you say when you offer help to a co-worker?

Talk about the picture.

- What do you think these women are doing?
- How do you think they feel? What makes you think that?

Key Words for Work

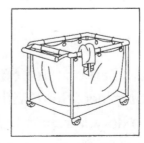

| table setting | dining room | hamper | tablecloth |

Getting Help on the Job

Peggy is a maid in a big hotel. She usually cleans rooms. Today she's working in a dining room for the first time. Nia is the dining room supervisor. Mary works for Nia.

Peggy: Excuse me. Are you Nia? I'm Peggy. Housekeeping sent me here.

Nia: Fine. The cart's over there. These tables have to be cleared. Reset them with eight table settings per table.

Peggy: I've never done this before. Could you explain . . .

Nia: I can't believe they sent me a trainee! This room has to be ready by three. If you need help, just copy Mary over there.

Peggy: She looks so busy. I don't like to interrupt.

Nia: You go ahead. I'm too busy to train you.

Peggy: Excuse me, Mary. I'm Peggy. I usually clean guest rooms. But today I was sent here. Nia told me to follow you around because I don't know what to do. I don't mean to interrupt you but . . .

Mary: Wait a minute! You can tell me your life story while we work.

Peggy: I guess I am talking too much. Well, what should I do first?

Mary: First, clear off all the dirty tablecloths and throw them in the hamper. When you finish, I'll show you how to drape the clean tablecloths on each table. Then I'll do one setting on each table and you can copy it.

Peggy: I think I can do that. Thanks for being patient.

Mary: It's no problem. Helping you makes my job easier.

Tips

Asking for Help with a Job
- Don't be afraid to ask for help.
- Make sure your questions are short and clear.
- Listen carefully when people explain things to you.
- Thank people when they offer help.

Check Your Understanding

A. Review the Information

Check ✓ **true, false,** or **NI** (no information).

True	False	NI	
_____	_____	_____	**1.** Nia is pleased that Housekeeping sent Peggy.
_____	_____	_____	**2.** Nia lets other people train new workers.
_____	_____	_____	**3.** Mary wants to become a supervisor.
_____	_____	_____	**4.** Peggy is embarrassed to ask Mary for help.
_____	_____	_____	**5.** Mary often trains new workers.
_____	_____	_____	**6.** Peggy doesn't want Mary's help.
_____	_____	_____	**7.** Peggy thinks she will be able to do the job.
_____	_____	_____	**8.** Mary has time to hear Peggy's life story.

B. Discuss the Questions

1. What kind of supervisor is Nia? What would you do if you had a supervisor like Nia?

2. Why is Peggy afraid to ask Mary for help? Have you ever felt embarrassed or afraid to ask your co-workers for help? What happened?

3. Why does Peggy talk so much? What are some ways in which people show that they are nervous or embarrassed?

4. How do you think Mary and Peggy worked together that day? Why do you think that?

5. Review the Tips for asking for help with a job. Which tip or tips does Peggy follow? Are there tips that she does *not* follow?

Which Would You Say?

Check ✓ the best answer to each question. Be prepared to explain
your choice.

1. Can you please show me how to change the vacuum cleaner bag?
   _____ **a.** I don't have time to stop and do your work for you.
   _____ **b.** I'm sorry, but I'm very busy right now. I can show you later.

2. Pardon me. Is this the way to the Tower Suite?
   _____ **a.** I'm not sure. Let me check with my supervisor.
   _____ **b.** I couldn't tell you. I'm new here.

3. There's an ink stain on the carpet in room 1228. What should I do?
   _____ **a.** Don't ask me! You can get in trouble for reporting problems.
   _____ **b.** You'd better call Housekeeping. They have stain remover.

What Are They Really Saying?

Read what Nia and Mary say. Write the sentences in your own words.

1. I can't believe they sent me a trainee!

   _____

2. Just copy Mary over there.

   _____

3. You can tell me your life story while we work.

   _____

4. I don't like to interrupt.

   _____

5. Helping you makes my job easier.

   _____

Try It Out

A. Asking for Help

Read each request for help. Decide what the person is really asking. Write the request in a shorter form. Compare your results with a partner or team. Make sure the shorter requests are still polite.

1. I'm sorry to bother you, but I don't know where to put the dirty tablecloths once I get them off the tables.

   _____

2. It looks like you're really busy, but I wonder if you could possibly show me how to use this cash register.

   _____

3. I hope you don't mind if I interrupt, but this is the first time that I've used this vacuum cleaner, and I need to change the bag, but I'm not sure how to do it.

   _____

B. Asking for More Help

Work with a partner. Read the situation. Discuss what each co-worker should do and say. Then create a conversation. Present it to the class.

You are a new employee in a busy video store. On your first day, you asked a co-worker to help you find some videos. On your second day, you still have questions. You don't want to interrupt or bother your co-worker too much. What's the best way to ask for help again?

Wrap-Up

A. Understanding Workplace Culture

1. Work with a team. Peggy was afraid to ask for help because Mary seemed very busy. The list below has some other reasons people give for not asking for help. Brainstorm more reasons.

> **For example:** I don't like to ask for help at work because

- • I don't know the best way to ask.

- • I don't want to bother my co-workers.

- • I'm afraid other people will think I can't do the job.

2. With your team, brainstorm a list of phrases or sentences that can make it easier to ask for help. Then share your ideas with other teams. Add other phrases or sentences that you would like to use.

> **For example:** Could you please check that I'm doing this right?

B. Application

Interview some workers. Ask them how they feel when they have to ask for help from a co-worker or supervisor. Ask what they say. Take notes. Compare your results with the class. As a group, decide if most workers speak to a supervisor differently than they do to a co-worker. Pick the best responses and add them to the list you made in part A above.

Work with a partner. Use the items on your list to practice making requests for help with your job or with activities you do at home or at school.

LESSON 12 Expressing Opinions

Objectives

- Express your opinion politely but clearly
- Listen and respond to others' opinions
- Express disagreement politely but assertively

Warm-Up

Talk about your experience.

- How do people at your workplace act when they disagree with a boss or co-worker?
- What do you do when you disagree with someone at work?

Talk about the picture.

- Who are these people? Where do you think they work?
- What do you think they are saying to each other?

Key Words for Work

magician

diner

waitress

advertisement

Making Your Point

Paula is a waitress at a diner. Gino makes the burgers. He never knows how many chicken-burgers to make. Sometimes he makes too many. Sometimes he doesn't make enough. The manager, Erik, wants to solve this problem.

Gino: How can I tell how many customers will order chicken-burgers today? I'm not a magician.

Paula: But we never run out of other specials. Why are chicken-burgers such a problem?

Erik: They're not really specials. We list our specials in our advertisements. But we don't advertise chicken-burgers. How can we tell how many we'll need each day?

Gino: Here's an idea. When I make 100 hamburgers, I'll make 50 chicken-burgers, too.

Erik: I understand what you mean. But that won't work. Some days we need 200 hamburgers and only 25 chicken-burgers. We need to know what our customers want.

Paula: What about this suggestion? We can count chicken-burger orders each day for one week. Then we'll know the average number we need each day. Gino can count the orders as he makes them.

Gino: No way. I'm too busy cooking. Counting orders is not my job.

Erik: I guess it's up to me. But let's do it for two weeks. Then we'll know if people eat more chicken-burgers on certain days.

Paula: I think we can all live with that.

Tips

Expressing Opinions
- When you state your opinion, be polite but assertive.
- Give reasons for your opinion.
- Listen to other people's opinions carefully.
- Make comments about the ideas—not the person.
- Try to reach solutions that everyone can support.

Check Your Understanding

A. Review the Information

Check ✓ the correct answer.

1. At first Gino wants to

   _____ **a.** be a magician

   _____ **b.** make more hamburgers than chicken-burgers

   _____ **c.** fight with Erik and Paula

2. Erik doesn't

   _____ **a.** care about Gino and Paula's problem

   _____ **b.** want to sell chicken-burgers

   _____ **c.** think Gino's idea is very good

3. Paula wants to

   _____ **a.** have Gino count the chicken-burger orders

   _____ **b.** find out how many hamburgers she serves

   _____ **c.** stay mad at Gino

B. Discuss the Questions

1. Do you think Gino, Paula, and Erik handled the problem well? Why or why not?

2. Gino says he can't do the extra work. What would you say if someone asked you to do something that was not part of your normal job?

3. Review the Tips for expressing opinions. Do you think Gino, Paula, and Erik followed the Tips? Give examples to show how they did or did not follow the Tips.

4. What can you tell about Gino and Paula's relationship from the way they talk to each other?

5. What kind of manager is Erik? How would you act if you were the manager in this situation?

Making and Responding to Suggestions

A. Do the Sentences Offer or Turn Down a Suggestion?

Check ✓ the correct answer.

	Offer a Suggestion	Turn Down a Suggestion
1. I'm afraid that's not what we need.		
2. What do you think about this?		
3. I have an idea. Let's try it this way.		
4. Unfortunately, I can't agree with you about that.		
5. That's a good suggestion, but I don't think it will work in this situation.		
6. Why don't we look at this solution?		
7. Here's a thought.		

B. Weak, Assertive, or Aggressive

Read each statement. Is the speaker being weak, assertive, or aggressive? Check ✓ the correct answer. Then share your choices with a team. Give reasons for your answers.

	Weak	Assertive	Aggressive
1. We'll do it my way, or I won't do it.			
2. Let's try it this way.			
3. I'll do whatever you think is best.			
4. Well, if you say so.			
5. I believe this will work.			
6. This is the only way to do it.			
7. I think we should try something else.			

Try It Out

A. Disagreeing Respectfully

Below are some poor ways to disagree with a co-worker. Match each one to a respectful way to say the same thing. Then add your own example to each column. Share your examples with the class.

Poor Way

_____ 1. That's the dumbest idea I've ever heard!

_____ 2. You need to get your facts straight.

_____ 3. I have a bone to pick with you.

_____ 4. Why don't you ever give an inch?

_____ 5. You can't really believe that will work!

_____ 6. _____

_____

Respectful Way

a. This requires some flexibility.

b. Maybe we can look at some other solutions as well.

c. I don't quite see how that will work. Could you explain?

d. Could we double-check that information?

e. I want to talk over a problem with you.

f. _____

_____

B. Disagreeing at Work

Talk to a friend or co-worker. Ask about a time that person disagreed with a decision made by a co-worker or supervisor. Take notes. Then discuss your results with the class.

Here are some questions you can ask:

• What was the decision? Why did you disagree?

• What did you say at the time?

• Would you say the same thing again? Or would you say or do something different? Why?

Wrap-Up

A. Understanding Workplace Culture

Work with a team. Discuss the questions.

1. Do some people make it easier for you to express your opinion? Who are they? What are some things they say or do to make you feel comfortable?

2. Think of a time you wanted to tell a group your ideas on a subject. Did you tell them? Why or why not? How did the group make it easy or difficult for you to express yourself?

3. Write a list of ways to state your opinion that you learned in this lesson. Brainstorm some new ways. For example:

   • Here's an idea.

   • What about this suggestion?

B. Application

Work with two partners. One partner takes Role A. One takes Role B. And one takes Role C. You are all at a meeting to schedule work hours. Give each person a name. Create a conversation. Try to find a solution that everyone can support.

Role A

You are a single parent. You took this job because the previous supervisor let you work flexible hours. You need to be home with your children every night.

Role B

You worked nights in this store for 15 years. Now you want more time with your family. You want to be home at night. You want to work the day shift.

Role C

You are a new supervisor. You were hired to increase sales. You need more workers on Monday and Thursday nights.

LESSON 13
Giving and Getting Feedback

Objectives

- Give constructive criticism
- Respond to criticism
- Use feedback positively

Warm-Up

Talk about your experience.

- How are you evaluated at your job?
- What have you learned from your evaluations?
- How do evaluations make you feel?

Talk about the picture.

- What are the men doing?
- What do you think they are saying?

Key Words for Work

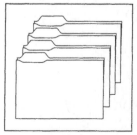

files

argue

evaluation

Giving Feedback at Work

Barry is a file clerk at a hospital. He is a very hard worker. But other things are as important as hard work. His supervisor, Rick, is giving him some feedback on getting along with his co-workers.

Rick: Barry, we have to talk. A few people have complained about you.

Barry: Someone complained about my work? What have I done? I work like a dog! I don't goof off! Who complained about me?

Rick: It's not about your work. Everyone knows you work hard. You even take on extra work. The problem is that you don't get along with your co-workers. You always argue with them.

Barry: Of course we don't see eye to eye! They're lazy and slow. They sit around talking. I do my work.

Rick: I know you do. But you have to get along with the people around you. You told me you want to be a supervisor. But good supervisors have to talk about problems without getting mad.

Barry: I know I fly off the handle. But no one listens to me. It just goes in one ear and out the other. What can I do?

Rick: Here's what I suggest. Why not take a course on communicating better? The hospital will pay for job-related courses. And you have to stop giving people a hard time. Then we'll talk about a supervisor position when you have your next job evaluation.

Tips

Giving Feedback and Evaluations
- Be clear about strengths and weaknesses.
- Be specific about what you want a worker to do.
- Set clear goals, and give clear rewards.

Check Your Understanding

A. Review the Information

Check ✓ **true, false,** or **NI** (no information).

True	False	NI	
_____	_____	_____	**1.** Barry respects his co-workers.
_____	_____	_____	**2.** Rick thinks Barry is a hard worker.
_____	_____	_____	**3.** Barry's co-workers like to work with him.
_____	_____	_____	**4.** Rick thinks Barry should study communication.
_____	_____	_____	**5.** Rick wants to get a better position.
_____	_____	_____	**6.** Hospital workers have to pay for job-related courses.
_____	_____	_____	**7.** Barry will get promoted at his next job evaluation.
_____	_____	_____	**8.** Barry wants to become a supervisor.

B. Discuss the Questions

1. Do you think Rick is a good supervisor? Why or why not? Why did Rick point out Barry's strengths first?

2. Barry uses strong language and gets angry. How do you think a supervisor should respond? How does Rick respond? What does that say about him as a supervisor?

3. How well do you think Rick and Barry get along?

4. If you worked with Barry, what would you say to him?

5. Rick gave Barry informal feedback in this conversation. How is a job evaluation the same as informal feedback? How is it different?

6. What do you think will happen at Barry's next job evaluation?

7. How does Rick use the Tips for giving feedback and evaluations to give Barry feedback on his work?

Understanding Idioms

Match the idiom in each sentence to the phrase that has the same meaning. Look back at the conversation on page 85 for help.

_____ 1. I work *like a dog.*

        a. get angry

_____ 2. I know I *fly off the handle.*

        b. have fun instead of working

_____ 3. Don't *give people a hard time.*

        c. They don't pay attention.

_____ 4. We don't *see eye to eye.*

        d. very hard

_____ 5. I don't *goof off.*

        e. think the same way

_____ 6. *It goes in one ear and out the other.*

        f. act unpleasant to people

Offering Advice

Imagine that your friend is not getting along with co-workers. You think the problem is your friend's fault. You want to give your friend some advice. What would you say?

Check ✓ the best answer.

1. _____ **a.** I don't want to hurt your feelings, but you could have a serious problem.

   _____ **b.** Boy! You've really made a mess of things!

2. _____ **a.** No wonder you can't get along with those people.

   _____ **b.** I think I see what might be causing the problem.

3. _____ **a.** Whatever you do, make sure your boss doesn't find out.

   _____ **b.** Maybe your supervisor could help you solve this problem.

4. _____ **a.** Maybe you can ask them to discuss the problem with you.

   _____ **b.** Oh, forget about it. You'll never be able to talk to them.

Try It Out

Responding to a Job Evaluation

Rick gave Barry this written job review at his next evaluation. Read the review. Think about what questions Barry had.

Work with a partner. Create a conversation between Rick and Barry about the job review. Present your conversation to the class.

ANNUAL PERFORMANCE REVIEW

Employee: Barry Graf
Supervisor: Rick Alvares

Date: 6/15/99
Position: clerk, Grade E

	excellent	average	poor
General Work Habits			
• knows work and hospital routines	✓		
• attendance and promptness	✓		
• accuracy of work	✓		
• completes work on time	✓		
• takes on extra duties as needed	✓		
Working with People			
• is helpful to patients	✓		
• gets along with other employees		✓	
• uses helpful criticism		✓	

Comments: successfully completed recommended course; improved relations with co-workers: continue support in that area.

Recommendation: Promote to supervisor, Grade 1; probationary period of one month

A. Understanding Workplace Culture

Interview some workers. Ask them what they think is the most important feedback they get on a job evaluation. Complete the chart. Compare your results with the class. As a group, discuss what information most people want to get from job evaluations.

Name/Job	Most Important Feedback
Abe Watts, lab technician	individual comments my supervisor writes; whether she will give me a raise

B. Application

Work with a team. Bring in a copy of a job evaluation form from your workplace. Compare forms with the team. What items appear on most or all forms? What items are special to some forms? Then brainstorm a list of the items your team thinks are most important. Create a job evaluation form.

Compare the form with other teams. Explain why your team included certain items. Explain how the form would give workers useful feedback.

UNIT 3 REVIEW

When you talk to co-workers, supervisors, clients, or visitors at your workplace, your speaking style varies. It may be informal or formal. Read each pair of sentences. Write *I* next to the more informal version. Write *F* next to the more formal version.

1. _____ **a.** Don't give me such a hard time.

   _____ **b.** Let's try to talk without getting mad at each other.

2. _____ **a.** It's hard for us to agree.

   _____ **b.** We'll never see eye to eye.

3. _____ **a.** Follow the same procedure that your partner is using.

   _____ **b.** Just copy what your partner does.

4. _____ **a.** I can live with that.

   _____ **b.** I think that might work.

5. _____ **a.** No kidding!

   _____ **b.** I'm surprised to hear that!

6. _____ **a.** I don't have time for that!

   _____ **b.** I'm very busy right now, but we can talk later.

7. _____ **a.** I'm sorry the report was late, sir.

   _____ **b.** Sorry about the late report.

8. _____ **a.** No way that will work.

   _____ **b.** I don't think that's going to solve the problem.

9. _____ **a.** I'm not sure what the answer is.

   _____ **b.** Don't ask me!

UNIT 4
Using Company Communications

In order to take advantage of opportunities at work, it is important to know the kinds of information that companies provide for workers. It is also important to know how to use the different ways in which that information is provided.

Think about how you get and share information at work. Do you receive written announcements or memos? Do you look at notices on bulletin boards? Do you take messages for others?

In this unit you will develop your understanding of common types of company communications. You will practice reading and responding to

- work schedules
- announcements on bulletin boards
- posted job openings
- company memos
- telephone messages

LESSON 14 · Following Schedules

Objectives

- Learn how to read and follow work schedules
- Understand the importance of following schedules
- Identify good and bad reasons for changing schedules
- Learn proper ways to make schedule changes

Warm-Up

Talk about your experience.

- What is your work schedule like?
- How important is it to follow a strict schedule at your workplace?

Talk about the picture.

- Who do you think these men are?
- What are they talking about?

Key Words for Work

cash register

alarm clock

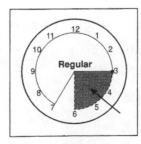

overtime

Following Company Schedules

Nasir is a new employee. Diego is telling him about work routines and schedules at Weber Cash Register Corporation.

Diego: It is very important to get to work on time at Weber. Your shift starts at six A.M.

Nasir: Six o'clock! I'd better not forget to set my alarm clock. It's so easy for me to oversleep.

Diego: Weber is serious about getting to work on time. A man on my old team was late 10 days in one year. Weber fired him.

Nasir: Fired him? That's awful!

Diego: Well, Weber has good jobs and pays good wages. So they can demand good work habits. But they are flexible in other ways.

Nasir: That's true. I like the flex-time work schedules. I'm going to work longer shifts on Tuesdays through Fridays. Then I'll have three days off.

Diego: That's what a lot of folks do. Oh, don't forget about calling in when you're sick. Call the shift supervisor before the shift starts. And if you take a day off for another reason, talk to your team leader early. Try to trade days with someone.

Nasir: Boy, there's a lot to learn! Is there much overtime at Weber?

Diego: We get lots of overtime in the fall and winter. That's the busy season. But not much the rest of the year.

Tips

Following Schedules
- Get to work on time.
- Tell your supervisor if you have to be late or absent.
- Know the right person to talk to about schedule problems.

Check Your Understanding

A. Review the Information

Check ✓ the correct answer.

1. At Weber, it's important to

    _____ **a.** change shifts every week   _____ **c.** fire workers who are late

    _____ **b.** take a day off each week   _____ **d.** get to work on time every day

2. Weber Cash Register Corporation

    _____ **a.** has a short workweek   _____ **c.** expects people to work hard

    _____ **b.** is always busy in June   _____ **d.** never pays overtime

3. Workers on a four-day workweek at Weber

    _____ **a.** work only in the winter   _____ **c.** have three-day weekends

    _____ **b.** never get paid overtime   _____ **d.** are the best workers

4. If you have to take a day off at Weber

    _____ **a.** tell a friend or co-worker   _____ **c.** do it only in fall or winter

    _____ **b.** talk to your team leader   _____ **d.** come in early the next day

B. Discuss the Questions

1. Why does Diego tell Nasir about the man who was fired by the Weber Corporation for being late? Do you think workers often get fired for this reason? Why or why not?

2. Does your workplace offer overtime work? What are the advantages and disadvantages of overtime for workers? For companies?

3. Why do you think flex-time scheduling is popular with workers? Do you think it is good for companies? Why or why not?

Understanding Schedules

This is the master schedule for the Weber Corporation. Each letter stands for a team of workers. Scan the schedule for information to complete the sentences below.

SHIFTS	Monday	Tuesday	Wednesday	Thursday	Friday
6 a.m. - 4 p.m.	A	A, B	A, B	A, B	B
9 a.m. - 5 p.m.	C, D	C, D	C, D	C, D	C, D
12 a.m. - 10 a.m.	E	E, F	E, F	E, F	F
4 p.m. - 12 a.m.	G	G	G	G	G

1. Nasir should try to join team _____ or _____ if he wants to have Saturday, Sunday, and Monday off.

2. Diego starts work at midnight. He works on team _____ or _____.

3. The 9 A.M. to 5 P.M. shifts work _____ days a week.

4. The 6 A.M. to 4 P.M. shifts work _____ days a week.

5. On Wednesday at 3 P.M., the four teams at work are _____, _____, _____, and _____.

6. A lot of work came in last Monday morning at 9 A.M. The shift supervisor asked members of team _____ to work overtime. They worked until noon.

Try It Out

A. Review the Master Schedule

Look back at the master schedule for Weber Cash Register Corporation on page 95. Decide which shift you would like to work. Then write the reasons that shift would be good for you.

I want to work _____ .

I like those hours because _____

_____

_____

Work with a partner. One partner will give reasons for wanting or needing to work a particular shift. The other partner will decide if those reasons are good ones. Then switch roles.

B. A Difficult Decision

Work with a partner. Read the situation below. Decide what the worker should do. Then create a conversation between the supervisor and worker. Present it to the class.

It is Friday at 5 P.M. You have been working since 9 A.M. You promised your family you'd take them to the movies tonight. The shift supervisor asks if you want to work four hours of overtime. You know that will add almost $75 to your next pay-check. You didn't take overtime last week. You're afraid your supervisor won't ask you again.

Now create a conversation between the worker and a family member. The worker explains the decision. The family member responds.

Wrap-Up

A. Understanding Workplace Culture

There are many reasons to ask for a schedule change or time off from work. Are the reasons below good or poor? Check ✓ the correct answer. Then add a good reason of your own.

Reason	Good	Poor
1. Your car won't start. You call your supervisor and say you'll be late for work.		
2. You want to take three sick days because your friend is visiting from your native country.		
3. You take two personal days because your child is sick.		
4. You have tickets to the World Series. You want to trade your day shift for a night shift for one week.		
5. You want to be home when your child finishes school. You ask to change from the afternoon to the morning shift.		
6.	✓	

Compare your answers with the class. Discuss the reasons for your choices. Then share the reason you added.

B. Application

Work with a team. Brainstorm a list of problems that people have following schedules. Then brainstorm ways to solve those problems. Compare your team's ideas with the class.

For example:

Problem
I often forget to set my alarm clock. So I oversleep.

Solution
Have a friend call at a set time and remind you to set the alarm clock.

LESSON 15 Understanding Announcements

Objectives

- Learn appropriate responses to various announcements
- Identify personal and work-related announcements
- Scan for information in announcements
- Learn where to find useful announcements

Warm-Up

Talk about your experience.

- What things can be posted on bulletin boards where you work?
- Why are those things important or useful to workers?

Talk about the picture.

- Why are these people looking at the bulletin board?
- What do you think they are saying?

Key Words for Work

pickup truck

cabin

dentist

circus

Reading Announcements

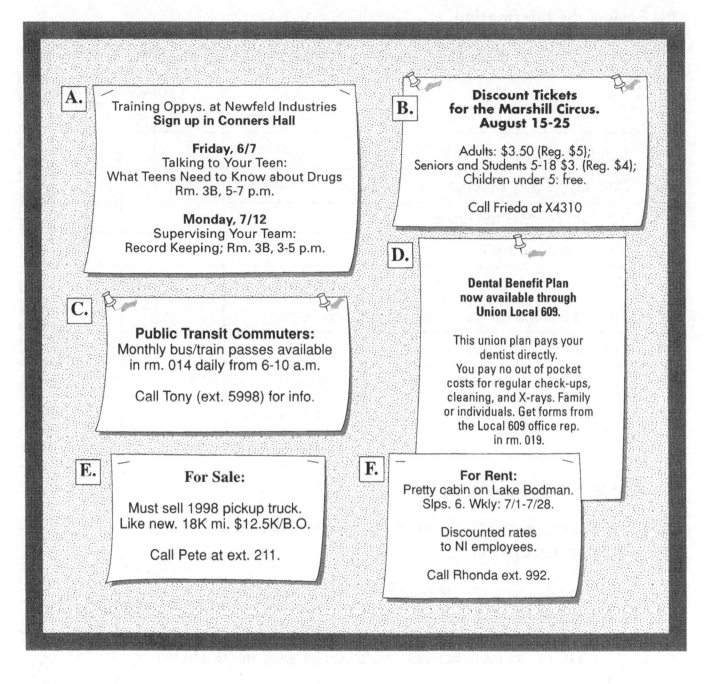

A.
Training Oppys. at Newfeld Industries
Sign up in Conners Hall

Friday, 6/7
Talking to Your Teen:
What Teens Need to Know about Drugs
Rm. 3B, 5-7 p.m.

Monday, 7/12
Supervising Your Team:
Record Keeping; Rm. 3B, 3-5 p.m.

B.
**Discount Tickets
for the Marshill Circus.
August 15-25**

Adults: $3.50 (Reg. $5);
Seniors and Students 5-18 $3. (Reg. $4);
Children under 5: free.

Call Frieda at X4310

C.
Public Transit Commuters:
Monthly bus/train passes available
in rm. 014 daily from 6-10 a.m.

Call Tony (ext. 5998) for info.

D.
**Dental Benefit Plan
now available through
Union Local 609.**

This union plan pays your
dentist directly.
You pay no out of pocket
costs for regular check-ups,
cleaning, and X-rays. Family
or individuals. Get forms from
the Local 609 office rep.
in rm. 019.

E.
For Sale:

Must sell 1998 pickup truck.
Like new. 18K mi. $12.5K/B.O.

Call Pete at ext. 211.

F.
For Rent:
Pretty cabin on Lake Bodman.
Slps. 6. Wkly: 7/1-7/28.

Discounted rates
to NI employees.

Call Rhonda ext. 992.

Tips

Reading a Bulletin Board
- Scan notices first to see what is posted.
- Carefully read notices that are important to you.
- Copy or take notes on information you can use.

Check Your Understanding

A. Review the Information

Check ✓ the letter of the announcement you would use in each situation.

	Announcement					
	A	B	C	D	E	F
1. You take the bus to work.						
2. You have a part-time job moving furniture.						
3. You just became the leader of a work team.						
4. You have a toothache.						
5. You want to swim and canoe on your vacation.						
6. There's drinking at your child's high school.						
7. Your family loves clowns and jugglers.						
8. You want to go on vacation with five friends.						
9. You need another vehicle, and you want a used one.						

B. Discuss the Questions

1. What announcements do you think were posted by the company? Why do you think that?

2. What announcements are related to work? What announcements are more personal?

3. Which of the announcements would you be most interested in? Why?

4. Why do you think people post personal announcements at work? Why do you think companies allow this?

Understanding Abbreviations

Match each abbreviation to its meaning.

_____ 1. oppys.

_____ 2. wkly.

_____ 3. 18K mi.

_____ 4. $12.5K/B.O.

_____ 5. ext. 211

_____ 6. reg. $5

_____ 7. X4310

a. regular price of $5

b. telephone extension number 211

c. $12,500 or best offer

d. weekly

e. opportunities

f. telephone extension number 4310

g. 18,000 miles

Looking at Announcements

Do the announcements below refer to company or personal matters?
Check ✓ the correct answer.

Company   **Personal**

_____   _____   1. Special Holiday Concert—Holmes Civic Center—Friday, 8:30 p.m.—$5 donation requested

_____   _____   2. Deadline to request change of work schedules: this Friday, October 10

_____   _____   3. Employee-of-the-Year Committee will meet Tues., Dec. 5 at noon in rm. 9.

_____   _____   4. Raffle to support Elmwood High football—call Rita, X 987, for tickets

_____   _____   5. For Sale: cellular phone/still in box. $50—firm. see Dan

_____   _____   6. Boiler Room 2 will be shut from 6 am to 10 am all week for maintenance.

_____   _____   7. Revised Policy Manuals now available—Please pick up your copy at the Front Desk.

Try It Out

Imagine you want your paychecks deposited directly into your bank account by Newfeld Industries. Scan this notice from the employee bulletin board. Use the information to complete the sentences.

DIRECT DEPOSIT PAYROLL OPTION

For the convenience of its employees, Newfeld Industries provides a program with many banks in the area for direct deposit of all or part of an employee's paycheck. To participate in the program, employees must fill out and sign a Direct Deposit Authorization Form. Details required are bank name and address and the employee's account number. This form must be accompanied by a blank check (write VOID on the front of the check). Submit the form to Personnel. Employees will receive a pay stub as a record of each deposit.

Copies of the form are available from Sandy in Finance, rm. 13

---

1. An employee must sign _____ to get direct deposit.

2. The form is available from _____ in _____.

3. The form requires certain information: _____

   _____.

4. The employee must turn in _____ along with the form.

5. Employees receive _____ as proof of the deposit.

Wrap-Up

A. Understanding Workplace Culture

Read the announcement from the bulletin board of Newfeld Industries. Then discuss the questions.

TUITION REIMBURSEMENT

Newfeld Industries pays 80% of tuition for job-related courses. To qualify for this benefit:

1. Get your supervisor's approval for the course you want.
2. Pay for the course. Get a final grade of "C" or better.
3. Give your transcript and tuition receipt to Personnel.
4. The reimbursement will appear in your next paycheck.

---

1. Do you think this announcement is important to many workers? Why or why not? Why must workers at Newfeld Industries get courses approved?

2. Why do companies provide classes or pay for a worker's education?

3. What courses would you take if your company provided or paid for them?

B. Application

Find out where people post notices and announcements. Look at your workplace or school, around your neighborhood, or in your building. Describe the kinds of announcements you found in each place. Compare your results with the class. Then make a class chart of places to find different kinds of announcements.

LESSON 16 Job Postings

Objectives

- Understand job postings
- Find out how to get information about jobs
- Assess skills and credentials
- Decide which jobs to apply for

Warm-Up

Talk about your experience.

- How did you learn about your job?
- How does your company let workers know about new jobs?

Talk about the picture.

- Why are these people looking at the bulletin board?
- Do they work here? How can you tell?

Key Words for Work

Position Open Apply Now!

Our busy company is looking for a hard-working individual with 2 + years experience to join our sales team. Please send resume and portfolio to Human Resources, Suite 16, 267 Meadow Drive.

job posting

receptionist

diploma

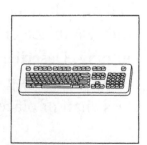

keyboard

Reading a Job Posting

Berta works in a health clinic. Her friend Hakim is looking for a job. He is talking to Berta about job openings at the clinic.

Berta: Hello, Hakim. Checking our bulletin board for a job?

Hakim: Hi, Berta. Yes, I heard there are new postings here every week. Now that I finished high school, I'm looking for a job here.

Berta: This is a good place to look. When I was looking for work, my neighbor told me about a job he saw here. What are your skills?

Hakim: I can use a computer and type 50 words a minute. Last year, I volunteered in the gift shop here. I ran the cash register and stocked shelves. I learned to deal with the public, too.

Berta: Look at this one: "Organized receptionist, part-time. Lots of patient contact. Good phone manner, some typing required. High school diploma required."

Hakim: That's interesting. I'll copy the job title and posting number. But I'd like a job with computers. I think it would pay better.

Berta: What about this? "Reliable data entry clerk for general clinic administration. Keyboard skills and spreadsheets are musts. Some college preferred."

Hakim: That sounds great. But I haven't started college. I wonder how much college is "preferred." I'll go to Personnel and find out. Meanwhile, let me know if you hear of anything else.

Berta: I sure will. The state unemployment office posts jobs, too.

Tips

Using Job Postings to Find a Job
- Match your skills and qualifications to job requirements.
- Copy important information from postings.
- Ask Personnel for more information about posted positions.

Check Your Understanding

A. Review the Information

Does Hakim meet the requirements of the two job postings? Check ✓
yes, no, or **NI** (no information).

Yes	No	NI	
			Receptionist
_____	_____	_____	**1.** be organized
_____	_____	_____	**2.** type
_____	_____	_____	**3.** deal with patients
_____	_____	_____	**4.** have good phone manner
_____	_____	_____	**5.** have a high school diploma
			Data Entry Clerk
_____	_____	_____	**6.** have keyboard skills
_____	_____	_____	**7.** use spreadsheets
_____	_____	_____	**8.** have some college coursework

B. Discuss the Questions

1. Why do people often apply for jobs at places where someone they know already works?

2. How did Hakim feel about the receptionist job? How do you know?

3. Why did Hakim want to find out more about a job that asked for "some college" when he knew he didn't have that qualification? Should you apply for a job if you don't have all the qualifications listed? Why or why not?

4. Why is it a good idea to let friends and relatives know you are looking for a job?

Understanding a Job Posting

Here is a job posting at an unemployment office. Read the posting and
answer the questions.

JOB OPENING

Admissions Assistant	Reports to: Head Admissions Clerk

1. Calls and checks insurance or Medicare information
2. Completes, checks, and connects patient ID bracelet
3. Completes patient information form and sets up patient folder
4. Brings patient to intake-floor administrative center
5. Transfers patient folder to intake floor clerk

- Friendly, out-going personality, detail-oriented a plus
- Some typing required, computer skills preferred
- High School diploma or GED required

---

1. What kind of company posted this ad? _____

2. What kind of work does the position require?

   _____

3. What kind of worker is the company looking for?

   _____

4. What qualifications are required?

   _____

5. What qualifications are desired? _____

Try It Out

A. Review the Job Posting

Look at the job posting on page 107. It gives only some
information about the job. Write questions you could ask to
learn other information you want to know about the job.

For example: Is this a full-time or a part-time position?

_____

_____

_____

B. Interview Questions

Work with a partner. Write questions that a job interviewer would
ask a person applying for the job described on page 107.

For example: Do you have any experience using a computerized database?

_____

_____

_____

C. Role-Play a Job Interview

Switch partners. One partner will play the job applicant and
use the questions written in part A. The other partner will play
the interviewer and use the questions written in part B. The
interviewer can create information that is not provided on
page 107 if it is needed.

After the interview, the interviewer can decide if the applicant
should get a job offer. The applicant can decide if he or she still
wants the job.

Wrap-Up

A. Understanding Workplace Culture

Hakim doesn't have a long work history. But he learned some important skills as a hospital volunteer—running a cash register, stocking items on the right shelves, and dealing with the public. It is often helpful to look at the skills you have developed outside of formal work and see how they can be turned into work skills.

Work with a team. Brainstorm a list of skills you have developed from volunteer activities or other life experiences. Then try to identify some paying jobs that use those skills. Complete the chart.

Volunteer/Nonpaying	Regular/Paying
dealing with public in hospital gift shop	dealing with patients as a hospital or clinic receptionist
taking care of brothers and sisters	taking care of children as a day-care assistant

B. Application

Interview some workers. Ask them how they find new jobs. Take notes. Compare your results with the class. Then create a class list or chart of ways to find jobs.

LESSON 17 Reading Memos

Objectives

- Understand memos
- Find details
- Clarify written information
- Compare job benefits

Warm-Up

Talk about your experience.

- What kinds of memos do you have to read at work?
- What job benefits can you get at work?
- What job benefits do people get in your native country?

Write a word list.

- What job benefits do you know about?
- What job benefits do you want?

Key Words for Work

vacation

sick days

holiday

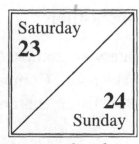

weekend

A Memo about Employee Benefits

Uni-Ply Manufacturing
MEMO

TO: All New Employees
FROM: Imani Woods, Training Director
RE: Job benefits

I will meet with all new employees on Friday at 11 a.m. We will review the company benefits listed below.

HEALTH PLAN Pick one:

- **Community Health** You can go to your own doctor.
- **HealthWise** You must pick a doctor from a HealthWise health center.

VACATION: After one year, you get 10 days vacation. After five years, you get 15 days vacation. You can save 5 unused vacation days each year to use in the next year.

SICK DAYS: You get 8 sick days each year. If you don't use them, you can save them from year to year.

HOLIDAYS: UPM is closed on New Year's Day (January 1), Memorial Day, Independence Day (July 4), Labor Day, Thanksgiving, and Christmas (December 25). If a holiday falls on a weekend, UPM is closed on Monday.

Tips

Understanding a Memo
- Read a memo once quickly.
- Read it again carefully.
- Ask questions about any parts that you don't understand.
- Put a check ✓ next to important parts.
- Identify any required action or response.

Check Your Understanding

A. Finding Details

Use the memo on page 111 to complete the sentences.

1. The meeting will take place on _____.

2. Ms. Woods is the _____ at UPM.

3. The _____ plan lets you choose your doctor.

4. Vijay was hired last year. He gets _____ vacation days this year.

5. Tanya was hired six years ago. She gets _____ new sick days this year.

6. Holidays are celebrated on a _____ if they fall on a weekend.

B. Discuss the Questions

1. Why do you think Ms. Woods put so much information about company benefits in the memo she gave out before the meeting? What do you think she will tell workers at the meeting?

2. Why is this memo important to new workers at UPM? What would you do in response to the memo if you worked at UPM?

3. Why do you think UPM lets employees pick their health plan? Which plan do you think is the better choice? Why?

4. What job benefits do you get? What benefits would you like?

Understanding Written Information

A. Can You or Can't You?

Read the memo on page 111. Decide if UPM employees can or can't do these things. Complete each sentence with the correct word.

1. You <u>can</u> pick one health plan.

2. You _____ go to your own doctor with Community Health.

3. You _____ save 10 vacation days each year.

4. You _____ keep all the sick days you don't use.

5. You _____ get a day off for Presidents' Day.

B. What Benefit Do You Use?

Check ✓ the benefit you would use in each situation.

	Health Plan	Sick Days	Vacation Days	Holiday
1. You go to a July 4th barbecue.				✓
2. You have the flu and stay in bed.				
3. You spend a week at the lake.				
4. You take time off for a baseball game.				
5. You get a medical checkup.				
6. You watch the Thanksgiving Day parade.				
7. You get an X ray for your son.				

Try It Out

Read the company memo. Then discuss the questions.

April 29

TO: All Employees
FROM: Frank O'Connor, Director of Human Resources
RE: Your Rights under the Family and Medical Leave Act (FMLA)

Come to an important meeting on Wednesday, May 5, in Conners Hall at 8 a.m. The company will explain updates on FMLA and the procedures for leave application. We will also explain restrictions on applying for leave under the FMLA.

Please bring your Employee Handbook to the meeting. You will receive new pages to add to it.

A second meeting will be scheduled to answer your questions.

1. What information does the memo include so employees can attend this meeting?

2. Why do you think the company is having a special meeting to give employees information about the FMLA?

3. Why do you think the company announced this meeting in a memo? Do workers need any other information before the meeting?

4. What do workers need to bring to the meeting? Why?

5. When will employees be able to ask questions about FMLA policies? Why do you think the company is dealing with questions in this way?

6. How can information about the FMLA help workers?

Wrap-Up

A. Understanding Workplace Culture

Pick a job benefit you want to know more about. Some possibilities are child care, vacations, sick pay, worker's compensation, retirement, savings plans, and tuition reimbursement.

Interview people in your class. Ask them how they feel about that job benefit. Find out if they want that benefit. If so, why? If not, why not? Complete the chart. Compare your results in small groups.

Benefit	Name/Country	Opinion about the Benefit	Wants It or Not/ Reason
child care	Lars/Sweden	costs a lot, not always good	No; wife takes care of children
child care	Maria/ El Salvador	very good; very expensive	Yes; has 2 children— she and husband work

B. Application

Bring in a memo from your workplace. Present it to your class. Give the important details of the memo. Explain the reason for the memo and why it was important to you and other workers. If the memo required an action or a response, tell what you did.

LESSON 18 Taking Telephone Messages

Objectives

- Learn how to take phone messages
- Give and ask for information politely
- Verify information in a message
- Use telephone message forms

Warm-Up

Talk about your experience.

- What kinds of messages do you take at home? At work?
- What things are difficult about taking a message?

Talk about the picture.

- What are the people in the picture doing?
- What do you think they are saying?

Key Words for Work

file cabinets

operator

catalog

office furniture

Taking a Message at Work

Suzanna Carlsen wants to order some office furniture by phone. She talks to two different operators at Master's Office Furniture.

Operator A: Hello.

Suzanna: Is this Master's Office Furniture?

Operator A: Yes, it is. Who do you want to talk to?

Suzanna: Well, I want to order file cabinets for PCI Stores. But I have questions about your catalog. Who should I speak to?

Operator A: Well, I guess you want Ms. Sherman in the Order Department. But she's in with the boss. That can take ages. Why don't you call back in an hour? No, wait. She'll go right to lunch. Call back at 1:30. She might be free then.

Operator B: Good morning. Master's Office Furniture. May I help you?

Suzanna: I have some questions about file cabinets in your catalog.

Operator B: You should talk to Ms. Rita Sherman. She's in a meeting right now. If you give me your name and number, I'll make sure she gets back to you as soon as she's free.

Suzanna: Thank you. Have her call Suzanna Carlsen at 311-8523.

Operator B: Call Suzanna Carlsen, C-A-R-L-S-E-N, at 311-8523.

Suzanna: Yes, that's right.

Operator B: May I ask what company you're calling for?

Suzanna: I'm with PCI Stores.

Operator B: Ms. Sherman will call you shortly. And thank you for calling Master's, Ms. Carlsen.

Tips

Taking Telephone Messages

- Give your name or your company's name right away.
- Record and verify important information in the message.
- Be polite and brief.
- Don't give personal information to the caller.

Check Your Understanding

A. Review the Information

Read the sentences and check ✓ the correct operator.

	Operator	
	A	**B**
1. asks Suzanna to call back later		
2. identifies the name of the company		
3. verifies the spelling of Suzanna's last name		
4. asks for Suzanna's telephone number		
5. isn't sure when Suzanna can get help		
6. gives Suzanna too much information		
7. thanks Suzanna for calling		

B. Discuss the Questions

1. What is the difference between the way the two operators greet Suzanna? If you made these calls, what impression of Master's Office Furniture would you get from each operator?

2. What does Operator A offer to do? What does Operator B offer to do? Which operator is more helpful to the customer? Why?

3. How does Operator B make sure the message is accurate? How else does Operator B follow the Tips for taking telephone messages?

4. Which tips does Operator A *not* follow? What advice would you give that operator?

5. Do you ever take phone messages at work? What do you say when you answer the phone? Which Tips for taking telephone messages do you follow?

Taking Messages

A. Completing a Message Form

Use information from the second conversation on page 117 to complete the message form that Operator B leaves for Ms. Sherman.

IMPORTANT MESSAGE

TO: _____

FROM: _____

COMPANY: _____

PHONE: (_____) _____

_____ please call back   _____ returned your call

_____ URGENT   _____ will call back

MESSAGE: _____

_____

B. Answering the Phone

Operator A is taking a call. Match each sentence to a better way to deal with a caller.

Operator A's Way

_____ 1. Hi. Who do you want to talk to?

_____ 2. Mr. Stevens is out sick today.

_____ 3. Give me your phone number.

_____ 4. What do you want?

_____ 5. You can tell him that when you call back.

Better Way

a. How can I help you?

b. I'm sorry. That person is not available today.

c. Would you like to leave a message?

d. Could you give me your name and telephone number?

e. Good morning. This is Master's Office Furniture.

Try It Out

A. Work with a Partner

Imagine there will be a training seminar at your job. One partner plays a trainer. The other partner plays a worker who calls the trainer. Each partner must find out the information below. Create a conversation between the worker and the trainer. Then present your conversation to the class.

The worker wants to find out

- if registration for the seminar is still open
- how many weeks the seminar runs
- what days the seminar will be held
- if there is a charge for the seminar
- what materials to bring

The trainer wants to find out

- the caller's name, department, and work extension
- if the caller has taken a previous work seminar
- the caller's supervisor
- the caller's work schedule
- how the caller learned about the seminar

B. What's the Message?

Work with two partners. Role A is the caller. Role B answers the phone and takes a message. Role C reads the message and responds. Give each person a name. Then carry out the actions described in the roles.

Role A

Make a call and leave a message. You want to set up a meeting with C. You can meet Monday or Tuesday before noon. You want C to call you back. Leave your telephone number.

Role B

Answer the call from A and take a message. Be sure to get the caller's name, phone number, and any message.

Role C

Read the message that B writes. Then do what A asks.

Wrap-Up

A. Understanding Workplace Culture

1. Work with a team. Brainstorm a list of tips that will help you take messages better.

   For example: Double-check the phone number of the caller.

   _____

   _____

   _____

   _____

   _____

2. Create a class chart. List the tips according to when they would be used. Some possible headings are

   • before you start

   • greeting a caller

   • during the conversation

   • saying good-bye

   • after the conversation

3. Work with a partner. Use your tips to role-play taking messages. Use experiences you've had in or out of the workplace, such as ordering supplies or finding out information about a job posting.

B. Application

Call a place that has a recorded message. Some possibilities are the public library, the INS office, a department store, a school or college, and a public utility company.

Take notes on the information you hear in the message. Include any important details. Share the message with the class.

UNIT 4 REVIEW

Use the words in the box to complete the sentences.

sick days	bulletin boards	call in	memo
benefits	reimbursement	schedule	verify
overtime	qualifications		

1. The _____ at this company include a health plan and a dental plan.

2. Will you get paid _____ if you work on the weekend?

3. If your _____ and skills match the requirements for this job, you should apply for it.

4. I'd like to _____ your address. Please repeat it slowly.

5. It's important to _____ and notify your supervisor if you are sick and have to miss a day of work.

6. The _____ at company personnel offices or unemployment offices are good places to look for a job.

7. Can you change your work _____ if there's an emergency at home?

8. My company sends a _____ to all employees when there is going to be an important meeting.

9. You can use your _____ if you have to stay home and take care of a sick child.

10. You will get a _____ for expenses when the company requires you to take a business trip.

Self-Evaluation

Review your beginning goals. Read the five goals you wrote on page 6. Copy them into the chart below. Then complete the chart to evaluate your progress.

| | Now that I have finished this book | | | |
	I do this better	I do this more often	I need to work on this	I don't do this anymore
1.				
2.				
3.				
4.				
5.				

Think about new goals. Do you have any new goals now that you have finished this book? Choose five new goals that are important to you now. Write them on the lines below.

1. _____

2. _____

3. _____

4. _____

5. _____

B. Think about the sentences below. Write why you agree or disagree.

   1. I talk at work more often now because I feel more confident about my English.

   2. I use written materials at work more often now because I feel more confident about my English.

C. Complete the sentences below. Then compare them with the answers you wrote for part B on page 6.

   1. At work, I now talk English with these co-workers and supervisors:

   2. These are things we talk about:

   3. These are things I can now read at work:

   4. These are things I can now write about at work:

   5. These are things I still want to learn so I can use English better at my job:

Answer Key

■ Lesson 1

Check Your Understanding (p. 10)
A. 1. d 　　　3. c
　　2. b 　　　4. b

Asking Questions about a Job (p. 11)
Possible answers:
1. Where can I find more metal sheets?
2. How do I inspect my work?
3. What information goes in the logbook?
4. Why do you use a logbook?

Another Way to Say It (p. 11)
Possible answers:
1. I want to check if I've understood you.
2. Where did you tell me to put it?
3. When I finish, should I lift the blade? Is that correct?
4. I think I understand what to do now.

■ Lesson 2

Check Your Understanding (p. 16)
A. 1. on 　　　4. off
　　2. off 　　　5. off
　　3. on 　　　6. off

Using Sequence Words (p. 17)
1. First, before
2. Next
3. After that
4. Last

■ Lesson 3

Check Your Understanding (p. 22)
A. 1. power switch
　　2. filter
　　3. warm
　　4. replace
　　5. latch

Follow the Steps in Order (p. 23)
5, 7, 4, 1, 9, 6, 3, 2, 8

Using Action Words (p. 23)
1. Lift 　　　4. Remove
2. Cover 　　　5. Rinse
3. Shake

Scanning Written Instructions (p. 24)
hammer, knife, level, tape measure

■ Lesson 4

Check Your Understanding (p. 28)
A. 1. true 　　　5. false
　　2. false 　　　6. true
　　3. false 　　　7. false
　　4. true 　　　8. false

Using Time Expressions (p. 29)
A. 1. last week
　　2. last
　　3. tomorrow
　　4. in a few days
　　5. a few days ago
　　6. days ago
　　7. yesterday
　　8. next week

Try It Out (p. 30)
A. Possible answers:
1. What room should I start in?
2. Do I have to fill the paper towel dispensers?
3. How many cartons of gloves should I order?
4. Do I have to do anything else?

■ Lesson 5

Check Your Understanding (p. 34)
A. 1. Santos 　　　5. James
　　2. Santos, James 　　　6. Melrose
　　3. Melrose 　　　7. Melrose
　　4. Santos, Melrose 　　　8. Chu

Finding and Using Details (p. 35)
A. 1. c 　　　4. e
　　2. a 　　　5. b
　　3. d

B. 1. Monday: 153; Tuesday: 147; Wednesday: 246; Thursday: 178; Friday: 85; Total: 809
　　2. $177.98

■ Unit 1 Review (p. 38)
Possible answers:
1. I want you to ask questions before you begin to work.
2. Inspect the edges to make sure that they are smooth.

3. I marked the items that I completed with a check.
4. Bandages get used up quickly.
5. Write a note about that in your logbook.
6. Do you understand that?
7. How much work did you finish today?
8. I think I understand what you said.

Unit 2

Lesson 6

Check Your Understanding (p. 42)
A. 1. c   3. d
    2. a   4. b

Categorizing (p. 43)

Gear	Body Part	Hazard
goggles	eyes	flying sparks
headphones	ears	noise pollution
respirator	lungs	chemical fumes

Try It Out (p. 44)
A. Safe near Machines   Unsafe near Machines
   work gloves   long hair
   goggles   loose sleeves
   hard hats   bracelets
   hairnets   dangling earrings

Lesson 7

Check Your Understanding (p. 48)
A. 1. a   3. b   5. a
    2. b   4. a   6. a

Safety Rules and Reasons (p. 49)
   1. b   4. c
   2. e   5. f
   3. a   6. d

Try It Out (p. 50)
A. 1. a, c, d   2. b, e, f

Lesson 8

Check Your Understanding (p. 54)
A. 1. false   5. false
    2. NI   6. false
    3. true   7. true
    4. true   8. false

Giving and Understanding Warnings (p. 55)
A. Possible answers:

1. Don't eat or drink anything from this container.
2. Put dirty rags in the trash can.
3. Always wear something to protect your hearing.
4. Keep this end up.

Shout It Out! (p. 56)
Possible answers:
2. Watch your head!
3. Put your head down fast!
4. Pay attention!

Lesson 9

Check Your Understanding (p. 60)
A. 1. true   5. NI
    2. false   6. NI
    3. NI   7. true
    4. false   8. NI

Try It Out (p. 62)
A.

METRO INDUSTRIES, INC.
ACCIDENT REPORT

Name of injured person: __Jaime__

Date of accident: _October 9, 2000_

Cause of accident: __Slipped on wet floor; didn't see warning sign; vision was blocked__

Describe injury (injuries): _fall on arm; head hit by carton; small cut_

Witness(es): _Subra_

Name and position of person completing report:
Irina, building manager

Unit 2 Review (p. 64)
Possible answers:
1. Always wear required safety gear.
2. You can prevent back injuries if you lift things carefully and follow some simple steps when you work.
3. If liquids spill, clean them up immediately.
4. Always use required safety gear.
5. Report accidents immediately.
6. Keep exit doors unlocked at all times in case of an emergency.
7. If your gear breaks, repair it or replace it right away.
8. Make sure that you can see easily over anything that you carry.

Unit 3

Lesson 10

Check Your Understanding (p. 68)

A. leader, tallies, manager, branch store, sales data, central office

Using Two-Word Verbs (p. 69)

1. try out
2. pick up
3. find out
4. finish up
5. send in

Lesson 11

Check Your Understanding (p. 74)

A.
1. false
2. true
3. NI
4. true
5. NI
6. false
7. true
8. false

Which Would You Say? (p. 75)

1. b
2. a
3. b

What Are They Really Saying? (p. 75)

Possible answers:

1. Don't they know I'm too busy to train a new person?
2. Do the same things Mary does.
3. Let's get started. You can tell me about yourself while we work.
4. I'm not comfortable interrupting Mary's work.
5. When I help you learn the job, you will do some of the work so I won't have as much to do.

Try It Out (p. 76)

A. Possible answers:

1. Where should I put the dirty tablecloths?
2. Please show me how to use this cash register.
3. Can you show me how to change the bag in this vacuum cleaner?

Lesson 12

Check Your Understanding (p. 80)

A.
1. b
2. c
3. a

Making and Responding to Suggestions (p. 81)

A.
1. turn down
2. offer
3. offer
4. turn down
5. turn down
6. offer
7. offer

B.
1. aggressive
2. assertive
3. weak
4. weak
5. assertive
6. aggressive
7. assertive

Try It Out (p. 82)

A.
1. b
2. d
3. e
4. a
5. c

Lesson 13

Check Your Understanding (p. 86)

A.
1. false
2. true
3. false
4. true
5. NI
6. false
7. NI
8. true

Understanding Idioms (p. 87)

1. d
2. a
3. f
4. e
5. b
6. c

Offering Advice (p. 87)

1. a
2. b
3. b
4. a

Unit 3 Review (p. 90)

1. a. I   b. F
2. a. F   b. I
3. a. F   b. I
4. a. I   b. F
5. a. I   b. F
6. a. I   b. F
7. a. F   b. I
8. a. I   b. F
9. a. F   b. I

Unit 4

Lesson 14

Check Your Understanding (p. 94)

A.
1. d
2. c
3. c
4. b

Understanding Schedules (p. 95)

1. B, F
2. E, F
3. five
4. four
5. A, B, C, D
6. E

Lesson 15

Check Your Understanding (p. 100)

A. 1. C   6. A
    2. E   7. B
    3. A or D   8. F
    4. D   9. E
    5. F

Understanding Abbreviations (p. 101)

1. e   5. b
2. d   6. a
3. g   7. f
4. c

Looking at Announcements (p. 101)

1. personal   5. personal
2. company   6. company
3. company   7. company
4. personal

Try It Out (p. 102)

1. a Direct Deposit Authorization Form
2. Sandy; Finance, room 13
3. bank name and address, account number
4. a blank check marked "VOID"
5. a pay stub

Lesson 16

Check Your Understanding (p. 106)

A. 1. NI   5. yes
    2. yes   6. yes
    3. yes   7. NI
    4. NI   8. no

Understanding a Job Posting (p. 107)

Possible answers:

1. hospital or clinic
2. check insurance, prepare patient information, transfer patient to floor
3. friendly, outgoing, detail-oriented
4. high school diploma or GED, typing
5. computer skills

Lesson 17

Check Your Understanding (p. 112)

A. 1. Friday
    2. Training Director
    3. Community Health
    4. 10
    5. 8
    6. Monday

Understanding Written Information (p. 113)

A. 2. can   4. can
    3. can't   5. can't

B. 2. sick days   5. health plan
    3. vacation   6. holiday
    4. vacation   7. health plan

Lesson 18

Check Your Understanding (p. 118)

A. 1. A   5. A
    2. B   6. A
    3. B   7. B
    4. B

Taking Messages (p. 119)

A.

IMPORTANT MESSAGE	
TO:	Ms. Rita Sherman
FROM:	Suzanna Carlsen
COMPANY:	PCI Stores
PHONE: (_____)	311-8523
✓ please call back	_____ returned your call
_____ URGENT	_____ will call back
MESSAGE:	has questions about ordering file cabinets from catalog

B. 1. e   4. a
    2. b   5. c
    3. d

Unit 4 Review (p. 122)

1. benefits   6. bulletin boards
2. overtime   7. schedule
3. qualifications   8. memo
4. verify   9. sick days
5. call in   10. reimbursement